From Hobo Flats to

The 5th Dimension

A Life Fulfilled in Baseball,
Photography and Music

LaMonte McLemore

AS TOLD TO

ROBERT-ALLAN ARNO

Dedicated to
my beloved Grandma Gertrude
and
my cherished mother, "Mama June"

CONTENTS

INTRODUCTION

"The sun rises and the sun sets for everyone. We're the only ones who screw everything up in between." That was the essential foundation for the many words of wisdom my maternal grandmother, a Cherokee Indian who never finished the third grade, nor could read or write, would offer in that way that was truly her own. Grandma was a stout figure with short smooth coal-black hair, warm hazel eyes, and an inherent sweetness in her knowing countenance. In my young mind, she was a presence. It's as if I never really looked at her, but I could feel her gaze, and when she spoke in her soft tones, the winds of time rushed into our humble home. Gertrude Whiteside was bestowed by heaven above with worldly vision, a virtual psychic gift of prophecy. Now, don't get me wrong. The way she looked at life was "Everything's so simple, why make it complicated?" She taught me, there is no such thing as a problem, only "situations." And I would say, "What?" And as years went on, and I really started to grow up, I realized what she meant. Simplicity was her brilliance. It was the embodiment of her all-embracing, loving heart.

With that being said, I have tried to live my life as simply as possible, and so it is with the writing of *From Hobo Flats to The 5th Dimension: A Life Fulfilled in Baseball, Photography, and Music.*

My friends and family say I have so many stories that I could write ten books, but I've chosen to take the best and put them into a memoir that I think you'll find equal parts historical, inspiring, and downright funny. Today, because of the Internet, I have friends from all over the world, too—loyal fans of The 5th Dimension, the legendary quintet I founded and sang with for over four decades, plus appreciative people who have followed my five decades of photography known as "The Beauty of the Week," in *JET* magazine.

The 5th Dimension was and still is known for bringing all kinds of people together in unity through our uplifting message of harmony. Marilyn McCoo, Billy Davis Jr., Florence LaRue, Ron "Sweets" Townson, and I were blessed to deliver Grammy-winning songs like "Up-Up and Away" and "Aquarius/Let the Sunshine In," which are considered anthems for a generation. The stories I'd receive about the effect our songbook had on people's lives, whether people heard a tune over the airwaves or in concert...I could write an eleventh book just about that! Here's one.

A man came to our show and told us after, with an urgent sense of gratitude, "I want you to know you saved my life!" With my curiosity piqued, he explained, "I was on a ledge, getting ready to jump off. My wife and kids were gone, I had lost my job. The police and firemen were trying to talk me down, but I had crossed my heart and was beginning the leap. Just then, 'Up-Up and Away' came on the radio. It was my favorite song. It was a sign, and as I started listening to it, they grabbed me and brought me back in." It sure redefines "Up-Up and Away"—literally. It makes me never take The 5th Dimension's "magic" for granted. I've heard from other fans who were going through difficulties as young people, even experiencing child abuse in their homes, and they've told me the positive spirit of The 5th Dimension was a saving grace for them, too.

On stages performing at the White House, headlining from Carnegie Hall to Royal Albert Hall, as a personal favorite opening act of Frank Sinatra, on TV's top shows from *The Ed Sullivan Show* to *The Flip Wilson Show*, from *Soul Train* to *The Tonight Show with Johnny Carson*, I always thought of making my grandmother proud. My goal was to do something I was respected for and would be remembered for—not to be just "a statistic," as is often said in regard to young African American men, but to make a difference.

I have friends, old and new, coming to me for advice to this day because of Grandma's sage-like words. They also insist I leave them with one of my "LaMonte tales," and I won't quit until I make 'em laugh. As I always say to them and now have the pleasure to say to you, "I don't make friends that I don't intend to keep. So now…you're stuck!"

CHAPTER 1

WORKIN' ON A GROOVY THING...OR THREE

"Now I want to tell you about how not to ever be bored..."

What is it that makes grandmothers so special? Maybe it's because they've "been there and done that" enough times to be a "specialist." I don't know where I'd be without mine. I had two sisters and a brother, but she stayed on *my* ass the most. When I finally got up enough nerve to sputter, "Why me?" Grandma calmly said, as if channeling from a higher place, "LaMonte, one day you will be in a position to take care of our entire family." I thought to myself, "This lady's crazy!" Well, guess what—I came to believe she should have been a fortune-teller.

By the time I got to my twenties, "Hobo Flats" became the endearing name my friends gave for any place I happened to live. I'd make my home a sort of a halfway house for anyone who had a dream or creative ideas... or just wanted a place to hang out and party. The door was always open to those who were willing to work on their attitudes, situations, and prejudices (especially the last one, because all races and nationalities were welcome). We accepted people who wanted to be accepted. We tried to find humor in everything and everyone, and believe me, no one was immune, not even "yo mama" ("Yo mama wears golf panties...eighteen holes!"). By the way, that harmless joke was courtesy of my buddy, Dick Gregory, who came to be known as a popular, politically-driven comedian. He, like so many in comedy, became a personal hero. I guess I realized at a very young age that a life without humor ain't no life at all. And Grandma helped me realize that life without purpose is plain boring. And if Hobo Flats is a state of mind, then its welcome mat should have a number three on it.

Before I explain more, I guess I should tell you some basics. I was born in St. Louis, Missouri, on September 17 (a Virgo), the first of four kids to June and Herman "J. C." McLemore. She was a housewife and maid, he was a janitor and sometime musician—a guitarist. My first memory of late-1930s America is that we lived in a garage in the back of a house that my mother cleaned, and we could use the toilet located on the back porch. My sister Merilyn, brother Donald, and I slept in a big dresser with its drawers pulled out, cushioned with pillows and blankets. We thought it was cool and called it our apartment—perhaps an early Hobo Flats! When my baby sister Joan was born, she slept on an army cot with my mom. I guess it was all too much for my father, because he left a note saying he couldn't hang no more and left—forever. Maybe my mom—a stately, strikingly pretty woman who we and everyone else affectionately called "Mama June"—cried, but we never saw it if she did. She just got more cleaning jobs and kept on steppin'. We then moved to a two-room house, and that's when Grandma came to help take care of us permanently, after my grandfather died. We moved a few more times (I guess when the rent was overdue!) We finally settled in South St. Louis between a meat packinghouse and the Monsanto Chemical Company, about five blocks from the Mississippi River, in a duplex with a funky outdoor toilet and a tin "number-two tub" hanging on the back porch. I hated that outhouse so much, I stayed constipated on the weekends until school on

Monday, when I could use their boys' room. One time, I took an overdose of Ex-Lax in anticipation. Lo and behold, while waiting for the school bus in snowy, ten-above-zero weather, the inevitable happened. Panicked, I boarded the bus; reaching the next stop seemed like an eternity as everyone started looking at each other. Not only was it the ultimate embarrassment when I was the one to jump off as the bus slowed down, but I had to walk all the way home feeling like a Fudgsicle.

Our neighborhood was a melting pot of people of all races even in a time of strong segregation. Poor people have one thing for sure in common: poor is poor. All we really had was each other, and for that reason I was never really taught prejudice. I just thought people came in four colors: white, black, red, and yellow. And if anyone was blessed to have something, they would share the best they could. There's pride even in the ghetto. When we didn't have much to eat, we would grease our lips with fatback so when we went out to play, we'd look like we'd just eaten. We were lucky enough to have a friend who worked at the packinghouse, and he would save all the parts that white people didn't eat—pig ears, tails, feet, hocks, and best of all, chitterlings (hog guts). At closing time, he would drop them out the window for us to catch. We were eating "low on the hog." Later I found out eating "high on the hog" meant ham, ribs, and pork chops. But as poor as we were, I never remember being hungry; I'm sure Mama June went to bed on an empty stomach many a night so her kids could eat.

Watching my mother breaking her back day and night as the only breadwinner, I wished I could do more to help. At nine years old, I got a job selling newspapers. The Sunday paper weighed more than I did! Mama June wouldn't take the fifty or sixty cents I made. The only real jobs for Blacks (then we were called Negroes) back then were as waiters, porters, and handymen, and if you were really fortunate, maybe you'd get a job at the post office. None of these really appealed to me when I was asked what I wanted to be when I grew up.

My true love was playing baseball. But that was impossible until Jackie Robinson broke the color barrier; even then it was farfetched. Surprisingly, my other love was taking pictures. Even as a boy playing cowboys and Indians, I had a cap gun in one holster, a camera in the other. But more about my photographic exploits later. The week the St. Louis Cardinals held an open tryout, me and three other Black guys went, not paying too much attention to the quizzical looks on the team members' faces when we showed up. They let us try out, and all the while we knew we had to run faster, hit harder, and eat more dirt…and we did. When I got home, Mama June asked how we did. I excitedly said, "GREAT, they're going to call us!" She plainly replied, "How, when we don't even have a phone?"

Every neighborhood seems to have a bully. One day a group of the guys were playing ball on a vacant lot near my house when Bull walked up (that's what we called him; to this day I don't know if he had a real name or not). I was batting, and my younger brother, Donald, who we nicknamed "Duck" (yes, think Donald Duck) was pitching. I asked Bull if he wanted to play. He nodded his big head no and then proceeded to walk up to Duck and ask for his glove (which actually was mine). With brooding entitlement, he began to reach for it. I ran up to him and exclaimed, "I can't go home without my glove!"

"Too bad," he sniffed, snatched the glove and knocked Duck down in one fell swoop. Well, no one touches my brother. Seeing red, I hit Bull with the bat I still had in my hand as hard as I could. We all ran, and Duck and I ironically hid under a police cruiser until it got dark. I was scared to death when I went to school the next day. I was soon amused to learn the whole school knew what had happened, and as a result, I was treated like a hero. The news from the grapevine claimed I broke both of Bull's kneecaps, and he would be in the hospital for a long, long time.

More than defeating the town bully, that baseball glove symbolized so much to me. It was my life's launching pad. I worked, scraped, stole, and

4

begged to get the fifteen dollars to buy it (probably a hundred dollars at today's prices). It was a Marty Marion shortstop glove (he was a St. Louis Cardinal star at the time), and the day I got it, I knew I'd be the envy of the neighborhood. I couldn't wait to show it off and play ball. Unbelievably, without warning a "monsoon" started, the hardest rain I'd ever seen. But nothing was going to stop me; I kept knocking on all my friends' doors to come out and play. They all thought my vigilant behavior crazy. When I got back home, Grandma saw beyond my soggy clothes. "LaMonte, I've never seen such a sad face," she observed then pressed gently as to what was really wrong. "I'm just bored," is all I could summon up.

She replied, "Son"—I knew her inimitable philosophy was coming—"let me tell you about boredom. If you ever trace the path of boredom, it will always lead back to you. If you stay bored all the time, you are a boring person." She continued, "As soon as you're tired of being bored, you won't be. It's OK to be bored, but be good and bored. Enjoy the moment and then get over it!" I was already getting over it. Grandma began her assignment. "Now I want to tell you about how not to ever be bored. I want you to pick three things that you want to do more than anything in life and don't bullshit yourself." Her expletives were rare and always came at a time to wake me up. She went on, "LaMonte, I know the first thing is baseball, and in a rainstorm like today, you can't play. Go to plan number two."

"Photography!" I spoke with conviction. When she inquired about number three, I had absolutely no idea. My follow-up assignment was to think about it seriously and get back to her. Sure 'nuf, about three months later, Grandma shrewdly, out of nowhere, piped up, "Son, now what's that third thing?" I freaked and lied and out came "Singing." I think she was as astonished as I was, especially since I had recently turned down her suggestion that I sing in the church choir. But I had just come from the street corner, where some of the guys from school were trying to start a group. They asked me to join in on the harmonies. I didn't take it too seriously, but I certainly liked how much the girls were giving us their undivided attention.

Believe it or not, to this day I can't remember ever being bored again...or giving way to defeat. And all three things turned out successfully. Here's my countdown: 1. Baseball—I was signed with the Dodgers farm system. When something unfortunate occured, it was on to the next plan. 2. Photography—I got to celebrate my fiftieth year as a freelance photographer for *JET* magazine. I have also photographed for *Ebony*, *People*, and *Playboy* and was even an early staff photographer at Motown Records. 3. Singing—I founded the multi-Grammy, Gold- and Platinum-winning quintet, The 5th Dimension. As the group's mellow bass, I glided through "The Age of Aquarius" with my colleagues in song for over forty years. And so, whenever I'm asked for advice from someone just starting out, I summon up Grandma's direct delivery. "Pick three things!"

CHAPTER 2

THE DECLARATION

"Sir…I don't shine shoes."

Mama June always taught me we have two choices: right or wrong. And I never wanted to be a statistic, remember? Well, I confess I nearly was…twice! I'm gonna be brief about this, not because I'm glossing over the truth, but because the aftermath of my poor decisions started a far more interesting saga. A cousin asked a few of us to hop a ride in what my instincts knew to be a hot (as in stolen) car. A night in the clink—let's call it guilt by association—was sobering, but not as difficult as making sure Mama June didn't find out. Thank goodness I was staying with her sister, my aunt Big, at the time, who knew I was relatively innocent and could keep a protective secret…and me from an ole-fashioned ass whoopin'! Next, getting involved for a moment with a bunch of fur-coat-wearin' St. Louis jive gangsters with names too funky for print, who wanted the lanky teenage edition of *moi* to "deliver some packages," wasn't a sharp move. When I got caught with the goods and nearly hopping a fence, this cop stopped me dead in my tracks…or rather on the fence. After his "freeze or I'll shoot," the surprisingly sympathetic policeman gave me the once over and said, "Pal, this life isn't for a guy like you.

You got two choices…jail or the military." Who knows, maybe Officer "Two Choices" was in cahoots with Mama June, but it was to the United States Navy I went like a bat out of hell, smack into the most challenging yet pivotal time of my life.

"I'm interested in photography, and I hear enlisting in the navy will provide me with a college education, sir," I sincerely told the recruiting officer. "Sure, sure," he responded. My first order on my first official day as a navy seaman was to shine shoes for a commanding officer—oh and to be a steward, essentially a cook and waiter for officers. I categorically refused…both. It got me on the bad side of some of the white guys, who deemed me an arrogant upstart, and some of the Black guys, who thought I was acting like a "bourgie, light-skinned cat."

"McLemore, did you finish shining my shoes yet? I'm getting ready to leave for shore," thundered the commanding officer.

"Sir, I was trying to catch you after you dropped them off for me, to tell you—"

"Tell me what?" he barked, detecting my patronizing tone.

"I don't shine shoes."

Yep, I lowered the boom! I didn't defy orders because being relegated to shoe shining or food preparing and serving was lowly and demeaning, nor because this was an act of racial discrimination that actually, a fairly recent ordinance had abolished. There was an even bigger reason. I required justice. I was raised to believe that all men are created equal. Grandma taught me, "Never look down on a man…unless you are tying to pick him up." No matter what troubles not obeying orders would cause, even the threat of being court-martialed, I was standing up for what was right… for everyone.

I thought my next step to get out of the now-revengeful commander's way would be to join the UDT (Underwater Demolition Team) division, which today is known as the US Navy SEALs. It was training to be "the ultimate warrior," doing ten times more than one would think the body could ever endure to survive. Jumping into an Olympic-size pool, or rather being shoved without warning off a diving board as high as an aircraft carrier while holding onto a life vest for dear life to keep from breaking your neck when hitting the water, and other special operations took their toll quickly. So it was back to…Alaska. Yep, that's where the spiteful officer who had it in for me shipped me off to. Alaska, land of the midnight sun…and no girls at the time, that's for sure.

One night a stir-crazy officer started sprinting down a runway with a flashlight in his mouth. Either he was truly "cray-cray," or was way too clever, for he got his leave quickly. A week later, a bunch of guys with flashlights in their mouths—an entire squadron, in fact—started running down that runway, too. They were promptly told they were geniuses but to turn around and cut the crap. There was no way out. That's one of the funnier Alaska stories. What wasn't was my run-in with rednecks, actually one particular jackass. In the barracks, it seemed as if he and his crowd were on one side, the Black guys on the other. If truth be told, that's how things were unfortunately divided. We were playing some Doo Wop Soul, he and his cronies started playing Country music and turned theirs up louder.

I said, "Man, we were here first," so I turned mine up louder. Then he turned his up louder. Pretty immature stuff until the air turned toxic and inflammatory. The redneck raged in a squeal, "Turn that nigger shit down!" Well, he was twice as big as me, but I had done my UDT training. I picked his big ass up and…BAM!

The military police came and questioned me, then they promptly put the jerk on lock-down for, quote, insulting my race. Where telling me to shine shoes was excusable, I guess the US Navy wanted to keep this incident down. Ever since that night, my back has never been the same. I mean serious stuff, where my doctors ask me, "How in the hell are you walking, much less still playing softball?" That's why today I'll run to first base but let someone run the rest of the bases for me. You may wonder if I think my knee-jerk reaction to the redneck's hateful ignorance was worth it. I was not out to hurt someone; I was out for justice, just like declining to shine shoes. Hey, I'm still getting to first base, so I'll let you decide the answer.

Post-Alaska, it was back to Oakland, where I finally got to do some photography...in the navy medical department. This is when cigarette research was just getting started. There was a comparison to be made between a young sailor who had been killed in a motorcycle accident— he'd never smoked—versus an old salt who smoked three packs a day for years. In the autopsy room, they had me photograph the dead men's lungs. The irony was I had just bought my first pack of cigarettes. I wanted to be cool. Everyone else was smoking at the time, even the movie stars, yada yada. You know the excuses! When I took a closer look at the cancerous lung under the microscope, looking like the devil itself, I tossed those cigarettes as far as I could throw them. Those shots of the healthy and un-healthy lungs are still floating around today in medical texts. The photos I took may have saved my life, as well as others'.

Way into my naval stint, my brother, Duck, wanted to come out for a visit, so the family happily chipped in for a train ticket, but upon his ar-rival, our sibling eyes met at the station with a "We forgot about where to stay!" look. I had a bright idea, as by then, I was working in the base's personnel office, signing people in and such. So I got him a card to get off and on the base and to get into the mess hall for chow. The finish-ing touch was to find one of the sailors who was just about Duck's size and borrow a uniform. We found one, and I boldly snapped a shot of my bro sporting his stripe and looking a bit like the cat who swallowed the canary! As I gave my younger brother the once-over, seeing him dapper in his uniform, I said, "Whatever you do, whenever you see an officer, just salute." I thought it would be a breeze for him to do so, just walking around until I got off work. But then I saw Duck coming down the street all puffed up, smiling and saluting everyone—and possibly everything—he encountered! I still don't know how we got away with it, and I guess I deserved the nightmares I had about it after my little brother's time as "guest seaman."

In Oakland I made the decision to become a naval airman. No jokes about "Up-Up and Away," please, but I thought it would "elevate" my prospects. I was so frustrated by then that I passed my qualifying test by parking a giant plane in one blind zoom. I literally closed my eyes and just nailed that baby right in its place. God was workin' overtime with that feat of back-parking! That's when I joined the baseball team, and soon it was the US Navy playing an exhibition game against the LA Dodgers! I was discovered there and was approached by the Dodgers about a contract with their farm team. After, when the guys took me out for a celebration…well, I wasn't a drinker, and that one beer I chugged got me just about drunk.

As we drove off from the speakeasy in a raggedy ole '39 Chrysler Royal, I must have leaned against the door handle, and I instantly fell out of the car onto my pitching arm. My tipsy mind was racing. "How could destiny be so cruel after all the effort I put into baseball? I've tried for so long!"

I was lying in the street as my buddies yelled, "Pull him out of the gutter before a car runs over him!"

"I don't care! Just let one roll over me!" I wailed.

Finally, when it was time to get out of the navy, I was asked, "Are you sure you won't stay? We know you want to be a full-time photographer for us, but if you re-sign, we'll guarantee that you go to college."

Pissed off, I said, "Four years here, and now I have to re-sign to go to school!" I felt like telling them to kiss my you know, but I stopped. I was grateful that in some way I got to serve my beloved country from 1952 to '56...and maybe make a difference, not only fulfilling my rightful duties, but for the times I stood up against what was unfair. Plus, I had confessed my accident and now-healed broken arm to the Dodgers, and they told me, "No problem." They still believed in me and would place me in their double-A league in Long Beach. I had promising new horizons awaiting. So I grabbed my $500 muster pay and bought—what else?—a camera.

Playing ball, taking photos, singing with local groups—juggling all three was sheer bliss. I'd run home in my Dodgers uniform after pitching, with no time to shower. I'd change clothes and get to music rehearsals, a bit sweaty but feeling like a winner. I was finally experiencing the true definition of "life, liberty, and the pursuit of happiness."

CHAPTER 3

ELEGANT DAYS,
JET-SET WAYS

"If there isn't a medium for gorgeous Black women, I'll create one."

"I'd devise my own magazine if I just knew an editor," I unabashedly expressed to this astonishingly beautiful yet horribly disappointed African American model after she, like so many, returned from a "go-see" I sent her on, rejected merely for the color of her skin. I never believed in obstacles—you know by now that Grandma instilled that in me. Rather, I simply thought, "If there isn't a medium for gorgeous Black women, I'll create one!" Ask and you shall receive, because it wasn't long after that I met John Daniels, a young editor who wanted to start a magazine.

We began brainstorming. "I know writers. Let them get the beat on promising Blacks on the college campus scene," said John.

"Celebrities! Let's go into their homes, too, and feature their decor and furniture," I offered.

"And show lots of fashion for both sexes!" we agreed simultaneously. And I knew wherever I was shooting attractive women, lots of men would inevitably congregate; Mohammad Ali, then Cassius Clay, had recently stopped by one of my shoots. It was always a party. But our goal was serious: to make a lifestyle magazine that catered to both Black women and men, and to make it elegant. *Elegant* was the perfect magazine title, but how to execute it with no money available whatsoever was the trick at hand. Well, here's the secret. You don't pay nobody, because as soon as you pay one person, you gotta pay everybody! So the writers, the illustrators, and the photographers all chipped in so John could have enough money to quit his day job and put it all together. John seamlessly laid it out with just plain ole white paper and tacked it together like a book until we agreed, "Man, this looks good 'n' yes...elegant!"

It was then on to finding a publisher...again, with no money. So I opened the phone book to publishers, slid my hand down the page like a magician and landed on Medallion Printers. "Let's try that," I thought. With two of my prettiest models, John and I went for a meeting, which went something like this:

Owner of Medallion: Looks great. How many issues do you want?

Me: Um...we'll get to that later.

Owner: Well, how much money do you have?

Me: We don't have no money!

Owner: NO MONEY! How do you expect to get a magazine together with NO MONEY?

Just as I was explaining we were willing to give up 49 percent, the owner's son passed by, spied our impressive dummy copy, and told his dad, "If all we have to do is print it, let's go for it!"

My old friend Belva Davis, who was by then a big television news commentator, held a reception for *Elegant* out of San Francisco. She knew everyone who was anyone there. Plus, we brought along our models, many who were from the Miss Bronze California pageant, the renowned beauty and talent contest of its day for Black women. That certainly sweetened the atmosphere. After sampling the sumptuous spread Belva had laid out, potential advertisers laid eyes on *Elegant*, exclaiming, "Wow, this is great…and you got full color, too. Who's the editor?"

Belva pointed to John Daniels. "Aw, he's just a kid. OK, then who's the photographer?" they inquired.

John pointed to me.

"Oh, it's another kid. You mean you guys put this together?" What they were really questioning was how we acquired all the major accounts like Coca-Cola and Dewar's Scotch that stood boldly alongside the extravagant-looking features. "I don't understand," they all seemed to scratch their heads. We didn't dare tell anyone that I'd straight out copied the ads from other magazines. I knew we'd eventually get nabbed, too.

Sure 'nuf, *Elegant* got published with impressive articles on stars like Sammy Davis Jr., Nancy Wilson, and Johnny Mathis, and every month it was marketed to someplace different. Statuesque, classically beautiful, café-au-lait-skinned, and vocally gifted, Marilyn McCoo was one of my models. She coincidentally had the same birth date as Mr. Mathis. Marilyn and I were dating at the time. It was a really old-fashioned relationship, where we respected one another and our talents, truly looking out for each other and our dreams. We'd talk of how someone like Johnny carried on the tradition of Nat King Cole before him, how his smooth groove crossed over, how much we admired that quality of connecting with people through pure class. And Johnny proved that to me personally when we interviewed and photographed him. While he charmingly accommodated the more established reporters from the Associated Press for the requisite amount of time, he asked *Elegant* to stay behind. He wanted to give extra attention to our fledgling Black-oriented magazine. "Let me do my share to help you guys get off the ground," he crooned with a speaking voice as soothing as his vocals, proceeding not only to give a tour of his smartly appointed home but to feed us—Johnny was quite the chef, too. This brotherly act defied the rather cold reputation of sunny Hollywood, where our first issue was actually headed.

By the way, when we circulated *Elegant* to different regions of the country, we purposely never had it dated, since we didn't know when the next issue would be coming out! And as predicted, we started getting these calls from the likes of Coca-Cola's law firm, Somebody, Somebody, and Somebody, saying:

Law firm: Is this *Elegant* magazine? Is this Mr. Daniels or Mr. McLemore?

Me: Yes, sir.

Law firm: We saw your magazine and noticed you're featuring an ad for Coca-Cola, and we just wanted to know who gave you permission to use our client's product.

Me: Well, sir, we wanted to talk to you about it.

Law firm: Damn right we're gonna talk about that. When can we set up an appointment?

At the meeting, I collectedly stated, "We had no rights to your ad, but we only wanted first-class products in our magazine. We charge five thousand dollars for a full-page advertisement, but since you're who you are, we thought we'd give it to you for free, to see if you liked it...and if you don't, we'll take it out." Well, we got the majority of those big advertisers, whose ads I out-and-out copied, to go with us…I mean, we certainly didn't have the money for them to sue us! In fact, it took some of those legal teams a few years to even catch up with us as *Elegant* continued to circulate cross-country and make positive waves.

It got so successful that we started *Elegant Teen*, and because I was a staff photographer at Motown's West Coast office by that time, I had access to all the early stars of the label's proverbial "Sound of Young America." I shot Marvin Gaye—a great guy who loved to play football and loved the ladies even more—at a rather raucous pool-party setting, although I managed to capture some sedate poses!

Then there was "Little" Stevie Wonder, the boy prodigy. Our photo session took place on the beach, where Stevie, complete with harmonica, asked me, "LaMonte, can you get me some wine?"

"You're underage, and I don't wanna go to jail," I replied loud enough for all to hear then whispered, "OK, but don't tell nobody!"

So we sat on the sand, sipping the grape, and to this day, every time I know someone is going to be seeing Stevie, I'll request, "Just walk up to him and say, 'Now, about that wine!'" Stevie always laughs. "Oh, it's that damn LaMonte, telling everyone!"

I also shot "A Day in the Life of The Supremes," with a very young Diana Ross, Mary Wilson, and Florence Ballard about town, shopping for and trying on tons of clothes, swinging on the park swings, and generally carrying on like sisters—there was not a bit of the tension evident that would later surface among these jovial three who were sincerely trying to make it. While Diane, as she was known to those close to her, was already the "featured singer," all the Soul brothers deemed Mary the sexiest… you see, Black men prefer a curvaceous figure! Regarding Miss Ross, far from the ravishing diva we've all come to know, I can never forget the back-in-the-day observation of one cat, who shall remain nameless: "Diane is nice enough, but she looks like a golf club with a wig on it!" Today, Mary and I are neighbors and remain close friends.

Inevitably *Elegant* and *Elegant Teen* took their final bows. Suffice it to say, we were young and still had things to learn; basically more money was going out than coming in. But to this day, I am proud of our being the only all-encompassing life-and-style magazine dedicated to African American women and men. There has really never been one like it. I'm also proud to display the richly toned covers and tear sheets of the magazine at art gallery exhibits across the country today as part of my legacy of photographic work. With panache, *Elegant* depicted a genuine representation of a glamorous, dream-promising, early-to-midsixties chapter in Black culture.

Near the time of this writing, there's another swan song that's appropriate to mention right here and now. The final printed edition of *JET* magazine, dated June 24, 2014, hit stands. Titled "An American Icon," it includes a young Florence LaRue in the "Beauty of the Week" retrospective and a toast to Marilyn McCoo and Billy Davis Jr.'s enduring marriage. As the premiere freelance photographer for *JET* for over five decades, this is a particularly sensitive issue for me. To be candid, now that *JET* will be going solely digital, it's like experiencing the death of a family member. And how many times were The 5th Dimension or our members featured on a *JET* cover? Countless times! To receive your *JET* was like getting a visit from a most delightful town crier. A staple in African American households, that little magazine was the go-to Black bible for current events and pop culture that spawned the quote, "If it wasn't in *JET*, it didn't happen!" Fans were often bemused to see the credit for LaMonte McLemore beside so many of the "Beauty of the Week" photos, a favorite weekly feature; it had them asking, "Is that the same guy, the tall one, who's in The 5th Dimension?" That's me! A kaleidoscope of memories flood my mind at times like these.

What led me on my path to *JET*? Well, when I got my muster pay and bought that camera, I forgot to mention I wound up on the Los Angeles City College campus. I'd tell the kids (especially the young women), who were only a little younger than me, that I was taking classes (which I wasn't!), and to just stand there and I'd take their photos for free. Then I'd come back to show the proofs, and they'd offer to pay, often four or five dollars a shot; the photos were that good. Voilà! I was developing my clientele. Later I did take some photography classes at the college, but the professor, liking my innovative ideas on how to position the camera and such, started having me teach his class. So I was basically never schooled in the art of photography. What gave me my epiphany was the chance to shoot at a dance studio. It was the dancers, the inherent composition of their moves, the very way their toes and even fingers were pointed, that became the backbone, so to speak, of the composition of my photos. Essentially, a woman's curves became the art, one of detail and balance.

Residing in Los Angeles with Duck for my first Hobo Flats experience, pitching for the Dodgers double-A league, and singing, I still needed something freelance to fill in the gaps. I answered a help-wanted ad in the paper: "Darkroom assistant needed."

"We need one for Christmas. Come right over for an interview," said the welcoming man on the phone. I was met with "The job's been taken."

"But I just called," I protested. Ha! I could hear the clerk telling the owner in the back, "That's LaMonte McLemore, and he's Black!" It was a white firm shooting white kids, but since they needed someone ASAP, they gave me a test shoot, which I promptly proceeded to ace. Soon I was no longer in that rather metaphoric darkroom but their top Christmas photographer, invited into homes with no bias due to my craft's reputation, including my easy way with getting cranky kids to pose. For instance, my gut told me to briskly roll a ball to what his parents warned was a particularly problematic brat. He rolled it back with a defiant yet accomplished ear-to-ear grin, and *snap*, it was the best picture of his young life! The little guy simply needed a break to strut his stuff, just like I did.

Then I met Cliff Hall, who convinced me to wangle a loan so we could start our own studio, and Hallmont (a combination of our names) was born. It was there that a stranger who turned out to become a friend for life, John Cook, God bless him, came in and said, "Why don't you submit pictures to *JET*?" Before I could respond, "Man, they got their own photographers…" he snatched one of my photos of a beauteous woman, and they wound up using it! Then *JET* asked me for some more photos, and the rest, as they say, is history.

The determined Sylvia Flanagan was the senior editor of *JET*, and she liked what I was doing. Before I arrived on the scene, they had three or four staff photographers. In the magazine, a bunch of strange pictures had surfaced with awkwardly posed models, even some with stretch marks! So Sylvia started using my photos primarily, as featured in the "Beauty of the Week." With fifty-two issues a year, as a freelancer I probably had 90 percent of the weekly editions, until the staffers started complaining to *JET*'s head honcho, its imposing, groundbreaking founder, John H. Johnson. "I think Mac and Sylvia have something going on. How come his pictures are getting the most exposure? We're staff photographers," they'd moan.

So a meeting was called, and Sylvia strategically asked for each photographer, including me, to submit six of our best shots. She turned all the slides over so our names weren't showing and when Mr. Johnson came in, she requested of him, "Before we begin, here are thirty pictures of girls. I'd like you to pick out the three pictures you'd most like to have in your magazine." He did so with quick instincts. Sylvia confidently instructed him, "Now turn them over." Well, all three pictures were mine. Upon seeing McLemore, McLemore, and McLemore, Mr. Johnson spat out, "Now why the f-ck are we having this meeting?" and walked out.

I think what appealed to Sylvia, as a proud Black woman, was the essence of what I was bringing to the table. I've noted that the dancers' stances became embedded in me. I wanted to bring out the best in those lines by celebrating the body. Therefore, I never promoted an anorexic model. I was a Black photographer shooting Black models, and to put it bluntly, since we are known for our behinds, if a girl came in with no butt, I was thrown for a loop. What's more, I traveled the world with The 5th Dimension, so I brought a global perspective. I eventually liked to push it to the limit and "bring the woman out of the woman." My signature became sexiness without being explicit—a sensual homage to diverse women of color. And don't get me wrong, that included their intelligence, intrinsic in their beauty. Later, at one of my gallery retrospectives, Sylvia, with her empowered yet thoughtful presence, called my work a "win-win."

When you take photos with the idea of heightening the elemental beauty of womanhood, you don't realize you could be changing history. I did know that when I'd literally be studying magazines like *Vogue* and *Glamour*, there were many ethnic models I was working with who would have done just as well as those who were being spotlighted in the major fashion magazines. Exasperated yet convicted, that's when I formed *Elegant* in the early sixties and received a type of full-circle confirmation circa '66, when I was asked to be a full-time photographer at *Harper's Bazaar* out of their West Coast office. I would have been the first African American in that position. In one way, it would have been awesome, because my prospects with the Dodgers had naturally petered out as a result of my earlier arm injury. But I turned the opportunity down because by that time, The 5th Dimension had newly formed...I mean, the other members had given up their day jobs, and I felt responsible.

But let me not jump ahead to "The 5th" just yet, because next is a vital stop for some "Hi-Fi nights." Ya know, Grandma used to say, "Take the gray out of your life and live ten years longer." She wasn't talkin' about hair rinse, but to not beat around the bush. No shades of gray, as in "tell it like it is." Be direct. So I reiterate, losing *JET* is like having a death in the family. And the best way to eulogize the vibrant weekly chronology it offered so many of us is to keep my own timeline movin' for you. I say with no gray, "Long live the memory of *JET*. I will miss you, with humble pride in knowing my contributions for fifty years to the 'Beauty of the Week' were an important part of your legacy."

CHAPTER 4

HI-FI NIGHTS 'N' FLIGHTS

"So poor Marilyn was back to sneakin', along with the rest of us..."

While my days may have been *Elegant*, my nights were strictly "high fidelity," for The Hi-Fi's was the Jazz-oriented vocal group I sang with in '63 and '64. Founded by original member Rex Middleton, who remained as our arranger, The Hi-Fi's featured two dazzling women, Marilyn McCoo and Fritz Baskett, plus three sleek cats: Harry Elston, Lawrence Summers, and dare I say, me! Our blend took us to places that evoke memories of everything from fleeing a hotel in the middle of the night to being managed by none other than the legendary Ray Charles. A blind man who never let it get in his way, Ray was a mastermind of fusing Rhythm and Blues, Gospel, Blues, Jazz, and even Country into Soul music. But it was his private plane, fondly nicknamed the "Gooney Bird," that was a pretty apt reference for the rollicking adventures our travels with him would hold.

After about a year of The Hi-Fi's getting favorable notices touring small clubs, Ray's manager, Joe Adams, got him to come over to Hobo Flats to audition us. "I've been hearing a lot about you kids. Go ahead and gas me,"

Mr. Charles, beaming, said in his gravelly yet sunny tone, the one Jamie Foxx captured so authentically for his Oscar-winning role in *Ray*. Well, we were living part of that story! Before we began, seemingly on cue, Joe put a book in Ray's hand. At first he held it upside down, then cocking his head as if realizing what he had done, Ray turned it all the way around. "Is this a trick, or does he really see?" I muttered under my breath as we began to go into the plaintive strains of "Lonesome Mood." Ray Charles signed The Hi-Fi's right after we hit our last compelling note and soon took us and our faithful conductor, Clarence McDonald, on the road as his opening act. It seemed unbelievable to have the opportunity to work with such a music pioneer, but believe me, Ray didn't pay us much of nothin'!

Our first official trip with Ray had us going up to Canada, by way of an initial gig in Pittsburgh, smack in the midst of a snowstorm. After we sang for our supper, Mr. Charles's private aircraft was only being permitted to depart Pittsburgh International Airport after the commercial planes took off…after our insufficient deicers left us with minimal frost on our wings. We got off the ground for only a few minutes before a deafening sputtering noise occurred. Soon came a clash, the door to the cockpit opened, and we could see a mountain coming up! We were lucky to stop thirty yards from it as we ran off the runway to avoid our rocky demise. Marilyn was first to jump up, with a resounding, "Give me my shit!" Coming from the quintessential "young lady," whose mother and father were both physicians, this request for her suitcases was quite amusing. We told Miss McCoo to sit down. She was actually quite the good sport, considering her folks were what the rest of us thought of as well-to-do, and she didn't have to tolerate flying less than first class…in this case, way less.

We remained in Pittsburgh a couple of days to repair the hydraulic system and check just about everything. When the plane was finally ready to take flight, with engines revving, Ray piped up rhythmically, "No, no, no, I don't know—something ain't right. Let me off the plane!" So there's Ray at the front of the Gooney Bird, tapping around. "What's this?" he asked the mechanics like a sly detective. It was the subtle knocking of a loose front landing pin that he discovered with his extrasensory hearing. If it hadn't been plugged in, and the plane had landed at a certain angle, the front wheel might have collapsed. So after that, every time we'd be ready for takeoff, we'd ask, "Hey, Ray, everything a'ight?" Leave it to the blind man to know if a plane is safe and literally sound. And to know just where to land, despite the lack of an FAA blessing. As in, one night Ray announced, "We have to make a little stop." I looked down to see no runway, then all of a sudden, car lights appeared. "Ah…ah, I'll be right back," confirmed Ray, who was soon getting some "product" out of this remote "airport." Ray got back on the plane, happy as a dog, while some guys pushed the plane all the way around at the end of the runway so we could take back off. Up in the air, during a rowdy game of poker that included Ray's renowned female backup singers, The Raelettes, cussin' 'n' fussin' over their bids, we hit an air pocket. Those tough-exteriored ladies were down on their knees real fast, begging in their most convincing church voices, "Oh, Lord, we'll do anything for you. Please just help us!"

One time, when we had just started with Ray but weren't quite regulars yet, The Hi-Fi's were invited to open for crooner Lonnie Sattin, who had singles out like "Soul Bossa Nova." Now, Marilyn's mother, Dr. Mary McCoo, didn't care too much for me at the time—OK, not me personally, but because I involved her daughter in a singing group that would take her away from her university studies. So the truly virtuous Marilyn had to sneak off with us! We had two cars—luggage in one, The Hi-Fi's in the other—to go join Lonnie in Chicago. We checked into our hotel feelin' all "sadity," as in full of our young selves. We got to the gig, and the club manager informed us, "Lonnie? He's not due to perform here till next week." So we slunk back to the hotel with no gig, no money, and with a very guilty Marilyn.

By the third day, the front desk rang with a "Y'all better come down and pay some money!" Luckily Ray had just flown into town for his own club date. We made the frantic call. "Mr. Charles, we're here…and we're stuck!" It was music to our ears when he scolded, "I told you kids to wait for work with me, but OK, I'll have enough room on the plane to get you home." So poor Marilyn was back to sneakin', along with the rest of us…down the hotel's fire escape! Leaving our suitcases behind for a quick getaway, we thought it was also "practical" to don our red sweaters with black vests and pants…our sole stage ensembles! As we boarded the plane, The Raelettes took one look at us and with hands planted firmly on their collective curvy hips, sniped in unison, "Well, la-di-dah, they even have traveling uniforms!"

As we continued working with Ray, we had a name change to "The Vocals." We even recorded "Lonesome Mood" on Tangerine Records. With Jazz not being tops with the record-buying public, the single probably sold five copies…because each of us bought one! On the road, the frugal Ray would drop us off at the town's fleabag, while he'd go to the proverbial Ritz. To save the little money we were paid, the girls would get a room together and so would the guys, but since you could only have two in a room, there was always an oddball. So as the two men would sign in, the other would just lag behind a bit and join us later. "They say we all look alike," we'd half joke. "Who's gonna be the wiser?"

One night in Boston, Ray dropped us off. Harry was hungry, so Larry and I went to our room, Marilyn and Fritz to theirs. While Mr. Elston got his sandwich, the motel closed its doors at midnight on the nose. A no-longer-hungry Harry began knocking at the entrance. "Who are you?" scowled a soon-to-be-off-duty employee, "Do you have a room here?"

"Well, I have some friends here," replied Harry, usually a fun-loving jester who seriously knew not to make waves; such was the climate of the times for Black people. Instead, he decided to get some discreet shut-eye in the lobby of another motel nearby.

I have one more story about Ray's Gooney Bird. There was a guy in the band who played a mean sax and was considered mean, too, as he was into black magic. I'm talkin' voodoo. We all had assigned seats on the plane, with everyone hoping to sit as faraway from him as possible. "Mr. Mean" called out to me, "LaMonte, I've been watching you. I think you're cool...c'mere and take a seat."

"Well, I think you're cool, too." I sidled up, trying to be...cool.

He continued, "Some of these guys, they don't treat me well, and when this tour is over, I'm gonna get 'em!" With that, he grabbed this bag of what amounted to dust and chicken feet. Wild-eyed, he ranted, "I'm gonna give that guy there rheumatism, give that other one there a heart attack..." and as he waved the bag in my face, he snatched it back with, "Now don't touch this, 'cause if you don't know what you're doing, you can mess yourself up!"

"Don't worry, I'm not gonna mess with your stuff...or myself!" I'm sure I replied, equally wide-eyed. As we dropped off band members on the way to California, we landed in Tennessee to learn one of the engines had been leaking. The engineer reported, "Good thing you stopped here, because if this ran out, you would have been in a whole lot of trouble!"

"Give me my shit!" Marilyn once again huffed. But this time I didn't chuckle. I knew it was time to move on. I recently had a dream about a newer, fresher group that put a hipper spin on what ours was doing. Yes, I saw it as clear as a picnic in the sunshine. Harry kept on with The Vocals, who merged into The Friends of Distinction, while Marilyn went my way. What I didn't see was the dawning of what would be called The 5th Dimension, and how it was going to come together like magic, not the voodoo kind...but like heaven itself.

CHAPTER 5

UP-UP AND AWAY—A TRAVELING SUNSHINE ODYSSEY

"The world's a nice place in my beautiful balloon..."

"How did the group get started?" is unequivocally the question The 5th Dimension was asked the most. It got to the point where we starting having fun with it in our act on stage and even during TV appearances like on *The Flip Wilson Show*. Here's how the "tall-tale" version went:

Florence (stepping forward coyly): In 1966, a bunch of young, clean-cut kids got together and decided to form a singing group.

Ron, aka Sweets (comes forward robustly): Now, Florence, you're giving the people a snow job. Let me tell you how it really was!

Me: Tell it like it was!

Sweets: Times were hard, we were all struggling. Florence had just graduated from college.

Florence: Uh, high school, honey!

Sweets: Anyway, she was teaching a bunch of second-grade kids. LaMonte, he was trying to be a professional photographer…could you believe with a fifteen-dollar Kodak flash camera? Marilyn, bless her heart, was out in Watts working with a bunch of young teenagers. And Billy, he was snatching jobs…

Billy: That's right!

Sweets: Purses, cameras, TV sets…anything he could carry off!

Marilyn: And what about you, Sweets? What were you doing?

Sweets: I was at my office on Wilshire Boulevard.

Marilyn: Yeah, the post office!

Sweets: Well, it's still an office…

OK, so here's my chance to tell you how it really was. It almost seems mythic by now. The three gents of The 5th Dimension all grew up together in St. Louis, Ron being a bit older than Billy and me. In fact, I had learned somewhere down the pike that my dad and Ron's had played guitar together at one time in an early Jazz combo! When both my St. Louis pals had come to Los Angeles to take their music further, I told Billy I had connections at Motown West, so to speak, since I'd been a staff photographer there a few years earlier. Billy, from an early age, was not only singing the best Soul, Blues, and Gospel in town but was managing

29

nightclubs in St. Louis, helping to promote other talent. He was a big hit overseas, too, while stationed in the army in Germany. While Billy would be waiting on his solo contract from Motown, my idea was to "persuade" him in the meantime to join my new dream concept for a group along with Sweets. I certainly knew Ron could sing the gamut of "classics" from Opera to American Pop Standards to even Doo-Wop! In fact, he was mentored earlier in his career by icons Nat King Cole and Dorothy Dandridge. Now, Marilyn, who according to our earliest bio "could sing before she could talk," was groomed for stardom from the start. She seriously studied the fundamentals with the best vocal teachers, including Eddie Beal, and took advantage of all of her high-school and college musical theater opportunities. Having a velvety tone, a multioctave range, not to mention a heartbreaking way with a torch song already made her a standout in our work with The Hi-Fi's. It was when I was shooting photos at the Miss Bronze California pageant that I first met Florence, the year's Grand Talent winner. Reflecting her acting as well as singing aspirations, she came out on stage with suitcase in hand, emoting "April in Paris" ("Avril en Paris") in French, no less, and it was the contest's judge, Eartha Kitt, who immediately purred, "That's our girl." I pretty much thought the same about this fetchingly petite alto, so I asked her to join the beauty contest's previous winner—who was none other than Marilyn!—with me and my St. Louis buddies to form what we'd first call The Versatiles. She was a bit reluctant, like all the others who were looking toward solo careers, so I convinced her and everyone to just come along as a hobby. Florence, who also had her teaching credential to fall back on, responded with sass, "If it's just a hobby, then why are you buying us outfits?"

In reality, my dream about the follow-up sound to The Hi-Fi's came together as a hunch. You know, people will put a group together based on a musical genre—Country, R and B, Rock—but all I knew was that these four very diverse people could sing and had a "look," and based on that, I blended my bass, and our one-of-a-kind style emerged. I took credit for it, but one could say it was essentially a mistake. I honestly knew nothing about putting a group together! In the beginning, and that date was actually October 1965, the other members were so far ahead of me that when we'd rehearse, I'd announce, "I'd like to take my songs home to work on them." The others didn't know I had a guy teaching me. We were in the basement, and he was tinkling the piano, and I was trying so hard that he finally said, "Are you sure you wanna sing?"

I was kick-ass determined in my response, "Shut up! I'm paying you, aren't I?" So I'd come back to rehearsal knowing my part, and I learned little by little, and that's how I essentially got comfortable singing. Luckily, later on when we all worked with our famed producer, Bones Howe—who had track records with Elvis Presley and The Association—and our gifted, Jazz-oriented vocal arranger, Bob Alcivar—who I was particularly close with—it wasn't like going to a job at all. Oh, I worked hard with Bones and Bob; even my backgrounds were learned akin to studying lead vocals, but the challenge of getting my part of those five-part harmonies just right became like hitting a home run!

Yes, the members of The Versatiles loved to rehearse, and we began booking small gigs to enthusiastic reaction, while starting, collectively to champ at the bit to be with the preeminent Motown as a group. Once again, because of my recent staff photographer position at their West Coast division, it was easy for me to connect. I did so directly with Marc Gordon, their senior VP who got Motown to give us songs to record—basically old Smokey Robinson compositions. We were left to our own devices to get them to the label's founder, the formidable Berry Gordy, who was still back in Detroit. Everyone in the group chipped in for me to take those demos to Berry, but each day when I hightailed it to Motown headquarters—you know, that historic l'il building that's now a museum—Berry would tell me, "I'm too busy, come back tomorrow."

I couldn't disappoint everyone, so by the third day, I planted myself on the Motown steps at 6:00 a.m., and when Berry arrived, he literally had to step over my long legs…if not ignore my plea, "Berry, if you don't listen today, I'm out of funds, and I'll have to leave by tomorrow!"

He shrugged without missing a step. "OK, come on in right quick!" His reaction to the recordings was, "Man, you all sound great, but I don't hear no hit. So just go back and cut some more."

So I went back. The group was terribly disheartened. However, the always even-tempered Marc Gordon revved us up. "If you go with Motown, you'll get lost in the shuffle behind The Supremes, The Temptations, and all…but the singer Johnny Rivers has this new record label called Soul City. He'll put y'all first. Plus, I got this writer I want you to listen to. His name is Jimmy Webb."

You see, Marc was leaving Motown and wanted to start repping us. So he arranged for a meeting of The Versatiles with Jimmy shortly thereafter and cleverly wondered aloud, "Now if we can just find a writer for you guys and also find someone to do Jimmy's stuff—"

Jimmy jumped up with, "Well, I am writing this song for a play…maybe you'll like it!" Barely out of his teens, Webb was a boy genius. Billy would tease him unmercifully about the holes clear through the soles of his sneakers. This cat was struggling! Well, we immediately loved singing Jimmy's Broadway-like tune, but it was so pretty, we didn't think it could compete with the radio chart toppers of the time. That song was "Up-Up and Away," and come to think of it, it's probably no mistake but divine intervention that its lyric included the line, "…we'll chase your dream across the sky." The dream continued when Marc formally began to manage us, and we officially signed to Soul City for our first album. For it, our new manager encouraged us to find a hipper moniker, even though The Versatiles described us well. It was Ron's methodical wife, Bobette, who transferred Sweets's idea about calling us The 3rd Dimension into recognizing each of our members. So The 5th Dimension was born. Some have told me The Fifth Dimension—although we spelled ours with the number—signifies the spiritual truth of all living things, transcending both time and space. We weren't quite thinking about that eternal concept back then, but damn, it sure sounds good if not appropriate!

We starting recording with Jimmy at the helm, and the record company asked each of us which song could be a hit. Everyone picked every other song off the album but "Up-Up and Away." With all the psychedelic-oriented music out there, Soul City chose it anyway, and of course it became the title tune of our first album. "Up-Up and Away" just seemed to soothe everyone in our restless country.

Our first big Top Ten hit soared like a "beautiful balloon" itself to number seven on the Pop singles chart. That summer of '67 in Marin County, California, we found ourselves on the same bill as The Jefferson Airplane and The Doors at the Fantasy Fair and Magic Mountain Music Festival. We thought we'd be out of place, but wound up performing "Up-Up and Away" to a standing ovation; in other words, our final "high" note went over well in the pungent, smoke-filled air! Yep, even the hippie audience grooved "under a twilight canopy" to what became our signature tune, one that virtually defined the upward momentum of The 5th Dimension's career. And the group won four Grammys for the song that also signified the start of Jimmy's tunesmith fame. Furthermore, it didn't escape me as we received our standing O at Magic Mountain, that only a few years earlier, I was given the assignment to photograph the troubling Watts Riots. I was starting to feel that maybe Dr. King's thought-provoking "I Have a Dream" vision had something to do with the sense of peace our music was providing.

And I'll tell you a secret. I bumped into Berry Gordy a few months after the tenth annual Grammy Awards ceremony, and although not yet televised, he quizzed me about the buzz our Song of the Year and Record of the Year awards created. "Yo, Mac, was that 'Up-Up and Away' *thang* on the demo you brought me?"

And I paused and said, "Why, Berry, yes it was!" I wouldn't dare tell him it wasn't and give him the satisfaction of passing up our quintet! I'd see Diana Ross in passing at Motown, too, and told her, "I also have a group."

"Oh, yeah, good," she'd say in her blasé way. I mean everyone told her about their supposed hit band. And then we were on *The Tonight Show*. Johnny Carson aired out of New York then, and she called me and said, "I know I didn't see who I thought I saw, LaMonte!"

"Well, I told you I had a group!" I grinned through the receiver.

"You didn't tell me it was that big!" shouted a "green-eyed" yet legitimately happy-for-us Miss Ross.

When we did Johnny, we were there to do "Up-Up and Away," with no major prepublicity at that point. Our famous "mod" designer-fashion statements, thematically designed by Boyd Clopton, were not yet part of the public domain. Even the eye-catching results of our photo sessions—where I'd often step in with my own photographer's eye to strategically rearrange The 5th's members to best show off our visual assets—had barely hit the press. So I walked out beforehand to scope the stage and caught an audience member saying, "I hear The 5th Dimension is Black!"

And I went back to the group and said, "People don't know we're Black!" The issue of our sound style was something that also evolved in people's perceptions, and I'd like to address that situation in the next chapter. What I'd like to point out here is The 5th Dimension was always invited on talk-show panels like Johnny's. In other words, we weren't solely asked to sing but to be ourselves, respected for what we had to say. Certainly it was another milestone, not only for Black vocal groups but for singers and musicians in general.

As I sat with The 5th Dimension on the guest panel, it was afternoon talk-show host Mike Douglas who asked with a twinkle in his eye, "LaMonte, has anyone ever told you that you look like a bronze Clark Gable?"

Marilyn and Florence chimed in, in harmony, "Yes, he's been told that!"

Well, after that I had to go look in the mirror. I had already looked at a couple of pictures of Mr. Gable, and I guess I could see where people saw that…I only wished I had his fame, his money…his everything! And yet I did possess gold; The 5th Dimension was amassing opportunities I could never have imagined, but I think my grandma in many ways predicted.

Ed Sullivan, host of the ultimate variety show, adored The 5th Dimension, and we made many memorable appearances on his Sunday night staple, *The Ed Sullivan Show*. In fact, we had an entire "5th Anniversary" show built around us, featuring our greatest hits. One time, lovable Ed—a bit medicated—stepped back on stage to applaud us exuberantly. The problem was, we hadn't finished our "Love Medley," featuring Bacharach/David's "What the World Needs Now," and The Beatles' "All You Need Is Love,"…uh, there was one more tune, "Have You Tried Love?" from our *Magic Garden* album! Loving comedy as I do, when The 5th Dimension appeared on *The Flip Wilson Show*, even before the group would go to perform our skits, Flip and I would be backstage telling jokes; those times were personal highlights. There's a scene where we're having a wild game of cards on an Orient Express-type of train—well, to this day when I play poker with friends like Mary Wilson of The Supremes, I think of that "actor's moment," and that it wasn't too far of a stretch! Glen Campbell, whose *Goodtime Hour* was a Sunday post-Ed Sullivan must-see, was a lot funnier than people gave him credit for. Glen spoofed his good-ole-boy image on our first network TV special, called "The 5th Dimension: An Odyssey in the Cosmic Universe of Peter Max," along with Flip, singer/dancer Joey Heatherton, and comic Arte Johnson. Fans still clamor for this one to be reissued on DVD, and I'll confess to recently viewing a bootleg of it (but don't ask me how I secured it!). Airing in May 1970, it was an adventure-a-minute musical ride—part the outrageous, quick-zinger format of the hit TV show *Laugh-In*, part Broadway's *The Wiz* before its time—through the set-design imagination of Pop art icon Max, produced by Ed Sullivan's son-in-law, Bob Precht. In fact, Ed appeared for the special's finale as a wizard of sorts himself, answering questions each of The 5th's members posed about romance, brotherhood, civil rights, and freedom…pretty weighty stuff, in the end.

Soon after, The 5th Dimension was invited to guest star on the episodic series *It Takes a Thief*, starring Robert Wagner as US secret intelligence Agent Al Mundy. Fans never seem to forget this one titled "To Sing a Song of Murder." Marilyn was featured as Marilyn Lee, entangled both in a bold-for-its-time romance with Bob's character as well as a plot to unwittingly blow up the president of the fictitious country, Rugeria. The latter entailed adding three odd chords to the end of "One Less Bell to Answer!" Because Marilyn's character was presumed dead at the beginning of the episode, we all took acting lessons to keep our reactions sharp; of course, we were already cool for the recording-studio segments featured. We studied with Beah Richards, the renowned African American actress, who actually had a small role on the episode. Many remember her touching performance in the movie *Guess Who's Coming to Dinner*, portraying Sidney Poitier's mother. When Beah began class asking each of The 5th Dimension's members what our goal was, I stated, "Just to count to ten." While Marilyn, Florence, Billy, and Ron looked on quizzically, Beah was nurturing. "Well, go on, LaMonte." I slowly counted aloud.

"One…two…" I could feel a sense of calm if not focus.

"Three…four…" The "movies of my mind" began flickering.

"Five…six…" My grandma's aura surrounded me.

"Seven…eight…" More peaceful warmth enveloped me.

"Nine…ten." My deepest sense of self prevailed.

I felt as if I had met my soul. Coming out of my meditative trance, I was touched to see most in the room, including Beah, had tears rolling down their faces. Like everything worthwhile, good acting is the definition of simplicity. And didn't Grandma always say, "Simplicity is perfection at its finest." I think simplicity is closest to God, and his reminding us to love ourselves just as we are, as he does.

I remember the opening theme to "The 5th Dimension Traveling Sunshine Show," our second network TV special, which aired in the summer of '71. It was "Light Sings," a single from the *Love's Lines, Angles and Rhymes* album. The song may have been a fan favorite, and I hate to disappoint anyone by saying so, but it was probably one of my least favorites of our songs. I know it was very pretty—that word again—but no one was going to be able to dance to it, and by that time, after our past successes with "Up-Up and Away" and "One Less Bell to Answer," I thought we needed the beat. From the Broadway show *The Me Nobody Knows*, our producer, Bones, was trying to recreate the sorcery of our very biggest hit, 1969's Platinum medley of "Aquarius/Let the Sunshine In" from the toast of Broadway, *Hair*. But that concept was past its prime. I don't think anyone in the group was crazy about "Light Sings" for that reason, except Florence, who always liked an airy tune!

The hardest thing about both our specials, as well as *It Takes a Thief*, was the work we put into rehearsing so we could be "present" as actors as well as singers for the tapings. These experiences served me well when The 5th Dimension starred in the road company of the Broadway revival of Fats Waller's *Ain't Misbehavin'*. This was in the mideighties, and the inventive management team of Sterling-Winters came up with the concept of putting us in such a show, to present a "new dimension" to our fans throughout the country. I was scared to death on opening night when I had to deliver my solo, "The Viper's Drag," with its inside dope references, out all alone on stage. But I received impressive reviews for the comedic flair I was able to inject into the tune. On closing night, the band members thought it was funny to inject something of their own—a "reefer" as substitute for the cigarette I dragged on as a prop during the song.

"I'm gonna kill you guys," I snickered when I discovered the pinched cigarette. But I couldn't be too mad, as we were finally done with the most hectic performance schedule The 5th ever endured. We were under the same strict union rules of Broadway, giving performances six days a week including Wednesday and Sunday matinees. We were probably paid more for one night of our regular 5th Dimension concert shows than doing a Broadway road tour for a full week, but I felt extremely accomplished for having tackled theater. The accolades I received, like "terrific interpretation," "packed with humor and sung with soul," and "no better proof of talent" as I "slithered across the stage cutting a dashing presence struttin' with my 'fines,'" from the *Pittsburgh Post-Gazette*, *Dayton Daily News* and *Flint Journal* respectively, were sparkling words I accepted humbly. Above all, I thought of how they would have made Grandma's eyes light up—the kind of "Light Sings" that matters.

CHAPTER 6

THE AGE OF AQUARIUS: THE MUSIC, DANCING IN MY MIND

"The Singer Tells His Story…"

"The Viper's Drag" reminds me to mention that no, I never smoked reefer, but it also calls to mind one of my all-time favorite songs The 5th Dimension ever recorded, Laura Nyro's "Black Patch," on our *Individually and Collectively* album. It always strikes me funny that one of my most remembered solo moments is the line I mischievously croon in full-on bass to punctuate Laura's Harlemesque panorama: "With lipstick on the reefer, waiting for a match." While the "invitations to my party" feel of "Black Patch" was the cream of the crop of our most soulfully styled five-part output, "How can you color a sound?" was my response to critics who implied that The 5th Dimension "sounded too white" by also approaching non-R and B musical genres. But Ron liked the line, so I was pleased when he began offering it in interviews, and coming from his classical vibe, the thought seemed pretty profound. I also wrote a personal account in *Playbill*. If I seemed nonchalant, I think I was only stating the obvious:

The problem was that we were doing something different than the Rhythm and Blues that most Black groups were singing. Well, we knew we could sing R and B, Jazz, and Gospel well, so we simply wanted to do something else. Now I think everyone understands what we're trying to do, and we never hear those complaints anymore.

Adding a soupçon of Broadway, a dash of Torch, and a pinch of light Opera to the mix of Pop-Soul, combined with our five individual styles, became a heady recipe. As such, our unique brand became known as "Champagne Soul"—I think some critic coined the phrase. I liked it, and we all started using it as a description of what The 5th Dimension did best. But back to the criticism we got in the late sixties. It was the era of Black Power, and the digs actually came from Black people themselves. It hurts when it comes from your own, but you understand it. Early on when we were opening for The Temptations, our very first single was "Go Where You Wanna Go," a slightly livelier cover of The Mamas and The Papas' Folk-oriented song that our record company thought we should undertake to establish ourselves. As we entered the stage smiling, dancing a form of the hitchhike while warbling, "You can go where you wanna go, do what you wanna do," the primarily African American audience basically re-acted with "Y'all can go where you wanna go…but just bring on The Tempts!" If I were in the crowd, I probably would have eye-rolled the same thing. For a while after that, I lost faith in us to the point where it almost broke us up, but our producer, Bones, told us in his sensibly soothing way to trust his vision. Being a visionary myself, I was in on the evolving Pop-Soul gamble, and so were the others as we harmonized in agreement to go with the flow. As a result, many, many patent-leather perfect hits slickly unfolded. Our recordings were supported by some of the finest session players of the day, known as "The Wrecking Crew," which included drummer Hal Blaine. And Bones often had us double our harmonies for a fatter wall of sound, which we liked to finesse by doing the overdubbing a few song bars at a time. It made The 5th Dimension sound recognizably head turning. But that one danceable hit that came to me in my dreams from day one, the one I think would have kept the original group relevant on the charts for way over our ten years together, never seemed to materialize.

After The 5th Dimension became famous, we were scheduled to give a concert at a historically Black college, and as soon as we arrived on campus and got off the tour bus, we saw students picketing. Thinking anti-Vietnam War sentiments were the theme, we soon realized no one was holding placards to "Bring Our Boys Home!" The protest was about us, as in, "We wanted a Black group to appear, and this is what they send us?!" Angry at such a scathing sentiment yet hurt underneath, my fellow members of The 5th Dimension wanted to speak up, but I was the one elected as emissary to address the "this ain't no Black group" bogus concern to the Student Union. In fact, I wanted to go. "We mean no disrespect, but we wanted a more soulful group," one student said as he greeted me.

"Have you ever seen The 5th Dimension in concert?" I countered. Even now, I'm provoked to think of our version of Sam Cooke's "A Change is Gonna Come," our good-time and get-down "Shake Your Tambourine," and our overall "Let the Sunshine In" live-stage-show concept that put a revisionist spin on the glorious goings-on of the club and cabaret scenes of the Harlem Renaissance from decades earlier.

"No, we've never seen your live shows," was the collective response.

"Well, then how can you be judging us? We especially should all be together. At least give us a chance to show you what we do," I said sweetly in my plea, but with an underlying sense of defiance. And so we arranged for all twenty of those Student Union members to have tickets to our show. Afterward, the leader came up to us with a tear in his eye, wanting a group hug. He then emoted the greatest line Marilyn, Florence, Billy, Sweets, and I could possibly hear: "We're so sorry we didn't give you a chance. Your show was fabulous!"

It's definitive moments like this that make me feel so satisfied in what we achieved with The 5th Dimension. We bridged cultural gaps and unified groups of age and racial diversity. The kids liked us, the parents liked us, and so did the grandparents. And like The Beatles, all our fans—regardless of race—knew both the first and last names of each of the original members of The 5th Dimension. Some people even referred to us as "The Black Beatles." Fans had their personal favorites, too, based on our likeability quotient. Marilyn was wholesome yet beautifully sophisticated, Florence was seen as a gorgeous, pint-size dynamo, Billy presented as outgoing and warmly winning, Ron, our "visual image" was lovably husky yet dignified, and I was thought of as...well, I don't really know what I was billed as by our followers, but I'll let you fill in the blank! I do know our original manager, Marc, made sure we were all known to the public for our individual personalities, and I was glad he received recognition for this in publications like *JET* and *Goldmine* at the time of his unfortunate passing in 2010. Marc and our producer, Bones, made sure that Country music fans who might not necessarily like Pop-Soul liked The 5th Dimension. Rock fans, the same thing. We got in the middle, and people would go that far, as in, "Well, I'll go to The 5th Dimension," whether buying our records, watching us on TV, or attending our concerts. And when all is said and done, it's really about love. You pray every night to be the best that you can be, you give out the love through your work, and when you get it in return, it provides a high that is sacred in nature. And I still feel that communion from the fans. The worldwide outpouring on my Facebook page for my birthday alone is mind-blowing! And that special love is a big part of what makes me as happy as I can be.

And now as a love letter to so many of you who have wanted to know my particular perspective as the group's bass, I want to give our six Grammys, fourteen Gold, and three Platinum records that you've given to us right back to you, from my heart to yours. Here's a "Mac-look" into The 5th Dimension's discography from 1967 to 1976—the albums, hit singles, "turntable hits," and even the least favorites I remember best. So as "Black Patch" asks, "People are you ready?" 'Cause Mac is "ready-ready!"

While our first album, 1967's *Up-Up and Away*, had a Folk-Rock vibe, I didn't realize until our second album, 1968's *The Magic Garden,* was completed that it was a musical masterpiece. That young prodigy Jimmy Webb arranged and conducted the songs as a suite—he had music pouring out of him—all about his love affair gone astray with a "flower child" named Susan. We worked so hard—sixteen hours on one of the tunes, "Orange Air." It was placed in such a high key, Jimmy kept saying it was flat, and when it came out, I think it was sharp...well, in a few places! Its astounding lyrics included:

> *I remember kissing her,*
> *that sad last night*
> *through the screen*
> *so hard I had a checkered mouth and nose.*

Jimmy's words were fantastical, other times heartrending, as with Billy's lead on "Requiem: 820 Latham." The lyric included scorching, achy phrases like

> *When we stopped the clock on that cold rock,*
> *mixed the hot young blood with granite dust*

Good Lord! And a lot of people didn't realize that 820 Latham is a street address, probably of Jimmy's muse, Susan, who I just bet greeted him "in that filmy thing and sat down on the porch swing!"

The Magic Garden remains an underground favorite all over the world to this day, here in the States, throughout Europe, and among our wonderfully dedicated Japanese fans. I know for Marilyn, Billy, Florence, and Bones, as well as myself, it is still our favorite album. There's another

Magic Garden song, "Carpet Man," and there's that high note at the end, "Carpet Ma-a-a-n!" Well, my little secret is that I'm not a true bass but a bass-baritone, so I hit that sucker out of the park, and I'm still amazed by my achievement! Oh, and there's a Beatles classic tacked onto side one of the album's song cycle, "Ticket to Ride," that was preproduced by Johnny Rivers before we started the *Garden* project. Some fans dig it, others find it out of place, but I always liked when the guys—Billy, Ron, and I—got to sing together. "Ticket" makes me "ride" into memories of what we'd do back in the day on the street corners of St. Louis. There was a feeling of brotherhood when the three of us would harmonize as members of The 5th Dimension, because we all grew up together—we fought and loved, laughed and cried, and worked and played together. Billy and I were in the drum and bugle corps. Ron and I both went to Sumner High School, where we teasingly called him "Danny Boy," as he would inevitably sing that tear-jerking standard at just about every event where he was asked to perform. Those early St. Louis days came right back to me every time I shared a mike in the studio or on stage with these men. With Ron no longer being with us, I cherish our recorded history all the more.

Stoned Soul Picnic, 1968's album bonded us to our megaproducer, Bones Howe, who in turn, introduced us to more complex, five-part harmonies, the prolific material of Laura Nyro, and even sexy songs like "California Soul" by Ashford and Simpson. When Bones first brought us the demo of Laura's "Picnic," I thought, "Finally, we can have a song people will dance to!" But then when we got into the studio, and I heard the arrangement, I thought, "Damn, this is the one song I wish were funkier!" Now, don't get me wrong, I think the world of Bones, and it was "a'ight," but I was just disappointed that our picnic didn't have more "flava" in its "sassafras and moonshine." Fans will probably notice that every time we performed it in concert, our conductor helped really kick it up. Even when we performed it on *The Ed Sullivan Show*, we all knew it needed that little bit of a bongo boost! But "Stoned Soul Picnic" did become a big hit on both Pop and R and B radio stations for its laid-back, "surry down" summertime groove, and somewhere along its chart climb, our first encounter with Laura Nyro dawned on me.

When The 5th was starting out, we were in San Francisco, rehearsing for a gig at a hip l'il place called Bimbo's. And we stayed in this hotel-apartment complex where the guys were in one room, the girls in another. As Billy, Ron, and I were rehearsing on the balcony, we heard this breezy soprano floating down from a cloud; actually, it was from the balcony above. We knew it wasn't either Marilyn or Florence, because they were two doors down.

"Hey," this raven-haired, Earth Mother-type called, "You sound good!" And we shouted up in unison with a touch of flirtation, "No, *you* sound good!" Yes, it wasn't until after we had a hit with her material that I realized Laura was the girl on the balcony...talk about "Sweet Blindness"!

I'd like to add that "California Soul" reminds me of two of my later favorites, the mystical "Love's Lines, Angles and Rhymes," by Dorothea Joyce, and that song with a great message about nostalgic loss but ultimate forgiveness, "Ashes to Ashes," by Lambert and Potter. You see, I call all three turntable hits. Nope, they really weren't danceable, and in my opinion, that's why they didn't sell enough, but the fans seem to have rather fervent feelings about them...and so do I!

Recording 1969's *The Age of Aquarius* album was literally like riding a fast-moving train...to the pinnacle of our career. To accommodate our tight schedule, we recorded it in Las Vegas while appearing with Frank Sinatra, a superstar with whom we had a mutual-admiration relationship. The recording studio was small, next to the train tracks; in fact, when a locomotive passed through, that clack got on our track! Take our voices off "Aquarius," and I swear, you'll hear that little train whooshing through. We didn't have time to redo it; we had to go back and open for Frank, so we left it...and it turned out to be our biggest hit in medley with "Let the Sunshine In."

The Aquarian miracle began with Billy losing his wallet in a New York City cab while we were headlining at the posh Royal Box at the Americana Hotel. Its finder called Billy, unbelievably happy to return it all, including credit cards and money, which was about two hundred dollars. To return the favor, Billy invited the good Samaritan to our show and afterward, the gentleman said, "Now I'd like to invite the group to my show." Well, he turned out to be the producer of Broadway's biggest blockbuster, that "American Tribal Love-Rock Musical," *Hair.* Marilyn, Billy, Florence, Ron, and I were seated separately—that's how hot a ticket the show was. After seeing Ronnie Dyson belt out "Aquarius" with such verve, we rushed toward one another at intermission shouting simultaneously, "We have to record that song!" Bones thought its "harmony and understanding" needed a little something-something more and tagged it with the upbeat "Let the Sunshine In" section of the musical's somber "The Flesh Failures." Bob Alcivar's special vocal arrangements for the group were in full swing with the girls' crystal-clear leads, and Ron and I getting to scale the charts. Then Billy came along, ad-libbing as only he could, inviting everyone to "sing along with The 5th Dimension." Irresistible, it became the Mount Everest of our chart history!

Our medley "Aquarius/Let the Sunshine In" was Number One in the spring of 1969 for six straight weeks and earned us two Grammy awards, too: Record of the Year and Best Pop Vocal Performance by a Group. It garnered a Grammy for Bones, as well. So I figure the $200 in Billy's lost wallet that was returned inevitably became $200 million for all parties concerned. It truly goes to show, in the spirit of the song's line, "no more falsehoods or derision, golden living dreams of vision," that honesty does pay. Oh, and did I mention the hit's timing in the scheme of things? With the first moon landing to take place that upcoming "Summer of Love," with its "When the moon is in the seventh house" beginning, "Aquarius" seemed to be precisely positioned to foreshadow Apollo 11.

Here's another example of a nifty sequence of events, and it brought us another Number One from *The Age of Aquarius* album. I confess, I was the one who told our producer that Marilyn and Billy had begun dating. Now I didn't realize "Wedding Bell Blues" was a Laura Nyro song Bones always loved and held onto, waiting for just the right moment. Seems my little tip prompted him to get Marilyn in the studio to sing the lead, which included that ideal lyric, "Bill, I love you so, I always will." In fact, Billy and the rest of us didn't even know about it until it was time for us to record the backgrounds! The song worked, too, because Marilyn and Billy were married shortly after the recording session.

Nineteen seventy saw us moving from the soon-to-be-defunct Soul City label to the shiny promise of Bell Records. *The 5th Dimension/Portrait* made for a perfect fresh-start album concept, as was bringing aboard famed sports artist Leroy Neiman to sketch us in action, rehearsing in the studio. From those renderings, he conjured up the stunning, energetically colored painting of The 5th Dimension that graced the aptly named project. We didn't have a lot of time to bond, but as I watched Leroy intently working on the sketches, I couldn't help thinking that I originally wanted to be an artist…and a journalist. I actually started out drawing when one day I realized taking a picture is worth a thousand words. Writing a song is like a snapshot of time, too.

> *Wanting to be together,*
> *yet wanting to be free,*
> *a love like ours could never be…*

That's the chorus of "A Love Like Ours," a song about a special woman in my life and the pull between staying home with her and the freedom of being on the road. The second verse goes like this:

> *Spend the days together,*
> *many things we start,*
> *and always the music,*
> *unfinished by the heart…*

If "The Girls' Song" from *The Magic Garden* was a sprightly sounding—but really, an apology—song from a woman's point of view, then my song, "A Love Like Ours," which vocal arranger Bob Alcivar put finishing touches on, was our bittersweet version of "The Guys' Song." Fans tell me it's a sentimental favorite to this day, and I'm pleased to have written it somewhere in the late sixties to find its rightful home on 1970's *Portrait*.

The multitalented Neil Sedaka provided us with "Puppet Man" for this album, and with its Rock-guitar licks, we turned that one out. Sedaka had also given us our follow-up to "Aquarius/Let the Sunshine In," a single I was partial to called "Workin' on a Groovy Thing." Overjoyed, Neil claims he almost fell off the couch when he saw us doing the tune on TV. For *Portrait*, our choice to make side two more of a protest record may have had some fans fall off their couches, too…in shock! Laura Nyro's Gospel-tinged "Save the Country" started our political statement. "The Independence Medley" followed. Using the exact words of the preamble to the Declaration of Independence, a friend of mine created a musical version called "The Declaration" that was featured in the play *Bread, Beans and Things*, and when I heard it, I brought it over to our concert arranger, René DeKnight. I knew The 5th could make it part of our message. Our producer, Bones, placed it in a medley with the potent "A Change is Gonna Come," culminating with The Rascals' "People Gotta Be Free." We soon came to find out that Armed Forces Radio wouldn't play "The Declaration," as they felt it depicted overthrowing the government! We did get to perform it in specially designed red, white, and blue attire on *The Ed Sullivan Show* and in formal wear at the White House for then-President Richard Nixon. "Tricky Dick," as he was nicknamed in the press, was no one's most admired president, but when the White House asks, artistic duty calls. And after we performed it, Nixon was the first to applaud for "The Declaration," breaking the stunned silence of attending politicians and dignitaries in the audience who surprisingly didn't know what to make of the self-explanatory lyric, "We hold these truths to be self-evident."

We were ready to move on from *Portrait* when a local DJ started playing "One Less Bell to Answer," written by Burt Bacharach and Hal David. The phones at the radio station began ringing off the hook, so we released it in response. Marilyn totally sang the drawers off this Jazz-Torch ballad that became not only a huge hit single for us on both the Pop and Soul charts but essentially our fans' all-time favorite song by The 5th Dimension. The "one less egg to fry" saga remains Marilyn's signature and one Florence blows the roof off, too, in concerts with The 5th Dimension today.

On 1971's *Love's Lines, Angles and Rhymes* album, Billy did a heart-wrenching job with "The Singer," a song I copenned with Elliot Willensky.

> *The singer searches for*
> *the perfect meaning*
> *in all the dreams that dance across his mind,*
> *laugh with him*
> *winter grows into spring*
> *cry with him*
> *lovers sing out of key, and out of time*
> *and nothing rhymes,*
> *and your life goes on*
> *in all of his songs…*
>
> ————
>
> *And if everybody loves the singer,*
> *then why oh why does the singer need love?*

My "poem set to music" composing style caught Frank Sinatra's ear, and when he strongly considered recording "The Singer," I was honored, but it was my good friend Gladys Knight who wound up cutting a nicely understated version of it with The Pips.

While 1972's *Individually and Collectively* presented our collective vocal goods like on "Black Patch," it also focused on the group members' individual interpretations, like Marilyn's solo of the catchy hit, "(Last Night) I Didn't Get to Sleep at All." Another proud moment of my vocal dexterity and the group's came from the album's "Sky and Sea," a wordless vocalese romp that was pure Jazz. It very much continued in the vein of another personal favorite, "Dimension 5ive" from *Portrait*.

The flip side of the singer's elation that "Sky and Sea" provided would be our recording of the title tune from 1973's *Living Together, Growing Together* album. I'll speak for myself (but probably for some of the other members) when I say it was the worst single we ever put out. "Living Together, Growing Together" came from a bomb of a movie, '73's musical remake of *Lost Horizon*, and we were strong-armed into covering it, as Bell Records was a subsidiary of Columbia Pictures, who produced the film. While we tried our best to put life into a basically bland choral arrangement for a soulless choir, even the tune's composer, Burt Bacharach, is quoted as calling the entire movie's notion a "giant bust." Conversely, besides the *Living Together* album's meaningful "Ashes to Ashes," I liked the "havin' church," revival-meeting feel of "Day by Day" from Broadway's *Godspell*, which we had the opportunity to present in our live concerts, too.

After the "Living Together, Growing Together" fiasco we seemed jinxed; we just couldn't find the right material for the next hit. People were bringing us boxes of songs, and even more songs, and we just couldn't find a thing. And I think that's what helped Marilyn and Billy make their decision to go out on their own. When Clive Davis took over Bell Records (which then became Arista) in '74, he made overtures about wanting to do things for us, make some changes. But Marilyn and Billy, our lead singers, really didn't want him getting involved, taking charge of our stuff. I think that might have been a youthful mistake, because Clive was getting ready to take us in another direction. I was getting ready to tell him I wanted something ultra-danceable, and I had a hunch he would listen to me. But I never got the chance. All we got was an opportunity to arrange some tunes for 1974's

Soul and Inspiration album. "Hard Core Poetry," another personal fave by the always socially conscious writing team of Lambert and Potter, was one of them. We also acquired a new producer for the *S and I* project, John Florez. His valiant quasi-Disco attempt for us, "No Love in the Room" was a single I asked myself if I'd buy and dance to…but it wasn't.

For 1975's *Earthbound,* we moved to ABC records for our final recording with The 5th Dimension's original lineup. It was a full-circle affair, as Jimmy Webb came back to produce the project, one I've found over the years to have a rather cult-like interest. Rumors have circulated about *Earthbound*, maybe because it took nearly forty years for it to resurface as a CD reissue. So let me answer the various odd questions that have cropped up for decades: Did we employ additional background singers for the album? Nope, and we never, ever have. We worked just as hard on *Earthbound* as anything we've ever done. Was there hostility in the air? Did Ron bring a gun to the recording studio? I think Jimmy said something to that effect in a Q and A, but if Sweets carried licensed protection, it certainly wasn't to intimidate any of his comrades in song! We were seasoned pros by that time, and if anything, we were all fighting for excellence. And finally, did Billy issue an expletive at the end of one of the songs, "I Got a Feeling?" Why yes, he did. It's one of Billy's wilder, full-throttle Rock 'n' Soul performances, and if I delivered the solo with such unbridled abandon, I'd utter "Shit!" at the end of the tune, too, as in, "What a blast!" When ABC Records (and the ever-observant Florence) caught it after the album's first pressing, since it wasn't fitting with The 5th Dimension's clean-cut image, the word was removed for the next pressing. What's more important about "Feeling" is that ABC was thinking of issuing it as a single. In fact, after a Friday evening concert at Westbury Music Fair on Long Island, we rushed to a TV studio in New York City to perform it on a telethon hosted by Geraldo Rivera. But Rock wasn't really The 5th Dimension's bag. More so, I think the main problem with *Earthbound* is that the album had nothing to do with the chart climate of the times. The first single chosen from it, "Walk Your Feet in the Sunshine," was a "Where did that one come from?" song for me. I felt we were stuck doing Bubble Gum, and it got to the point where, as the group's founder, I wanted to pick the tunes.

Soon after, Marilyn and Billy departed, and with their exciting replacements who had track records on Broadway, Marjorie Barnes and Danny Miller Beard, it was time to let "The new 5th Dimension" take wing in 1976. Like with *Earthbound*, there are some stories floating around about our next song choice, but I'll state here that it was my idea for The 5th Dimension to record "Love Hangover" from Diana Ross's album *Diana*. My heart raced as I said aloud to myself, "Finally, here's that really good dance record I'd been dreaming of!" As soon as I heard it on Diana's latest project, I zoomed it over to our manager, Marc, and he agreed that it could put us back on the map. We recorded it in a darkened studio for atmosphere, with Florence sensually cooing the breathy lead. Danny hit this supersonic note in the intro, and The 5th as a whole did some hot counterpoint harmonies throughout. It was becoming quite popular in the clubs here and in Europe since Disco and Dance music were all the rage; more important, it was climbing the charts globally.

Meanwhile, Miss Ross had released another song ("I Thought It Took a Little Time") as a single from her album. Diana was appearing in London, and my good friend Gil Askey, her conductor—a true gentleman who we recently lost—called me from overseas and related with shy if not sly amusement, "Hey, man, that song 'Love Hangover' that y'all did…"

"Yeah Gil, The 5th Dimension is thrilled with this one," I interrupted.

Gil went on, "Well, Diane called me while catching it on the radio and said, 'Good, I told Berry (Gordy) we should release that song as a single…uh damn, now wait a minute, that's not my f-ckin' song!'" Even the biggest Urban DJ in the country, Frankie Crocker out of New York's WBLS, had our single of "Hangover" going way up the chart until Diana allegedly told Berry, "Screw my current single! Stop that and put 'Love Hangover' out now! And whatever it takes, squash The 5th Dimension's record!"

So all of a sudden, our single—one we had just performed on Dick Clark's *American Bandstand*—wasn't played. Later, when Florence and I went to see Diane performing her acclaimed one-woman show on Broadway, *An Evening with Diana Ross*, she spied us in the front row, stopped dead in her tracks, and had the spotlight placed as if we were in a police lineup. As she pointed to a frozen Florence and me from center stage, she snarled with a smile, "Now, there's the enemy!" She was trying to be funny…but the lady meant business.

If The 5th Dimension's version of "Love Hangover" had been "the chosen one," we'd have been gone, as in back in the hit business. And to this day, I do think ours was better. I guess you can say, "I've got the sweetest hangover" still dancing in my mind.

Mama's motley crew—I'm in the center.

The McLemore siblings, L to R: Joan, Donald, Merilyn, LaMonte

Grandma and Grandpa fell in love while sharing his sandwich at the side of the train tracks.

L'il LaMonte holding Grandma's hand. I haven't changed much, right?!

In the US Navy, a smile through gritted teeth

Underwater Demolition, aka SEALs training. Watch out!

The Hi-Fi's, featuring me, Marilyn, Fritz, Larry, Harry, and founder/arranger Rex

With Mr. Ray Charles

The cover of Elegant magazine, and yes, so high-toned!

*"A Day in the Life of The Supremes"—Mary,
Diana, Flo (L. M. for Motown)*

Marvelous Marvin Gaye (L. M. for Motown)

First photo session (Liberty Records)

Autograph session: Clockwise, Ron (Sweets), Marilyn, me, Florence, Billy (center)

Sweets and I are gettin' ready-ready for a show!

Mug shot! (CBS)

Frank Sinatra was a fan of The 5th Dimension, and we were certainly fans of his.

Classic 5th—sophisticated, wholesome, hip (Arno Collection)

I captured Florence and Ronald striking regal poses in Turkey.

... and Marilyn coming from the woods

Florence and Marilyn, a Turkish dream, through my lens

We made the cover…many times! (JET magazine).

The visionary! From our TV special, "Traveling Sunshine Show"

The singer is a swinger...not!

"Have You Tried...Face Painting?"

Starring in "Ain't Misbehavin'"
(L to R, top to bottom: Sweets, me,
Michael, Florence, Joyce)

Florence and me with American
Bandstand legend and friend, Dick
Clark

At home in Vegas with golden memories

The Original 5th Dimension Nineties Reunion Tour—"Reunited and it feels so good!" (C A F)

*The Original 5th Dimension, getting our star on
the Hollywood Walk of Fame (Hollywood COC)*

*At my Beverly Hills photo exhibit, Ron,
Marilyn, Florence, Billy and me.*

Portraying the incomparable beauty of Jayne Kennedy is a photographer's blessing.

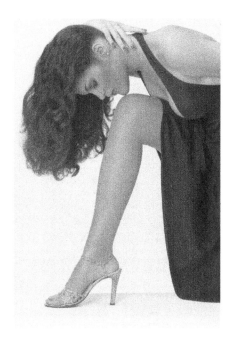

In photography, it's all about composition. Here, Jayne takes my work to another level.

My cherished grandma, Gertrude

Later photo of Grandma—her angel eyes follow me wherever I go.

*Tall 'n' sleek, Mama June in a
Western kinda mood*

*Mama June today, one hundred
years young, as radiant as ever.*

My beloved brother, Duck, looking like the cat who swallowed the canary or "borrowed" a navy uniform!

Sammy Davis Jr., "Mr. Show Business" and a wonderful friend

With the "Greatest," Mohammed Ali

With Ringo, a Fab 5 meets a Fab 4!

Forever friends, Marilyn, Billy, and me (Mieko McLemore)

With Robert-Allan Arno, a fellow visionary (Mieko McLemore)

High-Fiving with Billy as The 5th receive their star on the St. Louis Walk of Fame (St. Louis COC)

As a member of The Flashbackz (with a Z!)

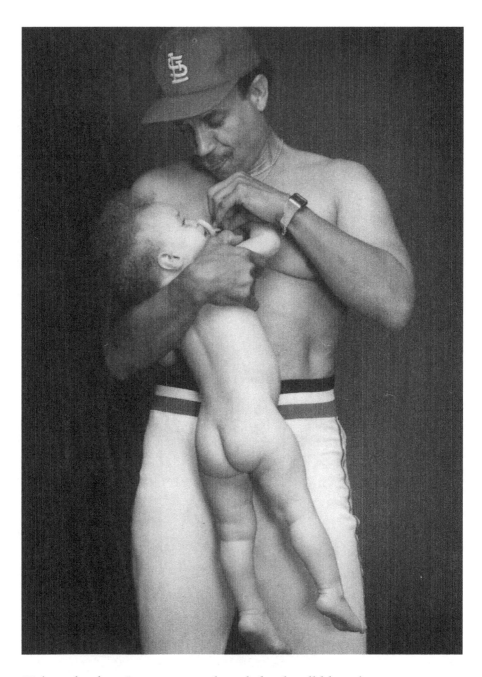

With my daughter Ciara, nine months and already tall like me!

My daughter, Ciara, follows in her mother's footsteps (and swimsuit) as a JET "Beauty of the Week."

Ciara has made me a proud grandpa of three, L to R: Raya, Shane ("L'il Mac"), and Makayla, with David Padover.

Dodgers farm team days

Senior softball every day keeps the doctor away.

A Love Like Ours was meant to be, with my lovely wife, Mieko.

(All photos unless otherwise noted: the LaMonte McLemore Collection; Cover photos: Tux—Benny Clay, The 5th Dimension—Arno Collection; Back cover: John Cook)

CHAPTER 7

PEOPLE GOTTA BE FREE

"All the world over, so easy to see..."

It seems the "Go Where You Wanna Go" thread in my life—wherever I've gone, whatever I've wanted to do—was underscored in the finale part of our "Independence Medley" from the *Portrait* album: "People everywhere just gotta be free."

After being aware of our standing-room-only performance at New York's prestigious Carnegie Hall in April of '73, the Department of State, under the US Cultural Presentations Program, invited The 5th Dimension to go behind what was then known as the Iron Curtain to perform our concerts and workshop with the schoolchildren of that part of the world. We waived our salaries and US bookings, making our nine-city tour of Turkey and Eastern Europe a national public service. The Goodwill Tour had us giving concerts in Ankara and Istanbul, Turkey, Bucharest and Ploesti, Romania, Warsaw and Katowice, Poland, and Ostrava, Bratislava, and Prague in Czechoslovakia. While we were fortunate to act as ambassadors, I was struck by how the meaning of freedom resonated in each city in either subtle or obvious ways. Billy observed with a regretful laugh that our albums in that corner of the globe were solely available as bootlegs. Florence later noted to Don Cornelius and the *Soul Train* kids, who were asking us questions about the trip, that our Eastern European brethren were not interested in knowing about our being Black Americans per se but were eager to know about our overall lifestyles, including food and fashion, as well as our educational system. Marilyn reported they inquired about everything from America's drug problem to our latest dance moves, which we showed off on stage.

Beforehand, our concert song list was scrutinized—it was "Jesus Christ Superstar" that was of concern to the officials and subsequently removed from our act. One night we all felt the "shadowing" of a mysterious trench-coat-wearing figure as we foraged for a bite to eat, making us feel as if we were in an episode of *Mission: Impossible*! Surely those slick members of The 5th Dimension were up to nothin' no good in Bucharest...not! At least no one could fault me for taking advantage of some exceptional photo ops of the gang. There's a classic shot of a regal Florence with a vested, Buddha-like Ron, poised on rocks against the Ottoman-era backdrop of Turkish architecture. My photo was set to run in *Vogue* but ended up becoming a fan favorite as featured in one of our souvenir tour booklets. Our trip culminated in not only a press conference with the Overseas Press Club, but our being the first entertainers to be featured on TV's politically oriented *Issues and Answers*. I recall the smitten interviewer telling Marilyn and Florence they possessed "voices like angels" as he asked us about how it felt to be so exceptionally lucky. The 5th Dimension was extremely blessed in our freedom to fly as artists "all the world over," I quietly contemplated as the broadcast ended with the relevant strains of our vivacious recording, "Save the Country."

Our concert vocal arranger, René DeKnight, was the one who got all the members of The 5th Dimension, sans Ron, involved in est (Erhard Seminars Training) around '73. What attracted me when I went to a meeting was that the founder, Werner Erhard, never said, "We are the best" but "We are what we are, and you can take it from there." And I liked that we could form our own opinion. Taking est was one of those major things that changed my outlook on life; simply put, it was about being aware. It taught me how to be present. And that whatever you are going to be, be the best at it. If you're gonna be a bitch, be the best bitch in the world! What changed for me after est was to know that I am in control of myself. Many have heard about attendees of est not being allowed to go to the bathroom over the course of the four-hour seminar. Basically, the motivation was "Don't let piss take over your brain, you tell your piss when you wanna go!" There's that "Go Where You Wanna Go" theme, again...I mean, if you can't discipline yourself, if you've really gotta go, then keep on goin'...home! We were asked to sign a list that was placed at the front of the room indicating if we had a medical problem, because then the stakes were different. Werner looked at the sheet of paper and said, "I have a class of two hundred people, and one hundred and eighty-five have a piss problem! This class isn't about bullshit, so you can come up here now and change that bullshit!" Only fifteen attendees remained on that list, those who really had a "condition." René wound up getting certified and became one of the directors of est. He must have told the powers that be, "Nothing bothers that damn LaMonte, so I want you to straighten him out," because I could always tell I was being singled out. In fact, I was told to stand in front of the class. While things proceeded, the instructor got in front of me and began to stare unrelentingly in my face. While this had happened to other students who began to cry and shake, I kept smiling, winking, and making faces. Finally, after twenty minutes I was told to sit my ass down.

If my language is a bit salty in describing my est experience, maybe that's the type of bold freedom of expression it elicits, although I hope I haven't offended anyone! And who knows, although Marilyn and Billy are strongly faith-based people today, est may have served as some sort of catalyst to awaken in them the freedom of challenging themselves to new musical adventures; they departed The 5th Dimension a few years later, in late

'75. I think est gave Florence and me the fortitude to carry on as she and I, along with Ronald, considered others to fill Marilyn's and Billy's vacancies, taking The 5th Dimension in exhilarating new directions. You may not know that the up-and-coming popular songstress Phyllis Hyman was considered as Marilyn's replacement; with her crisp diction, creamy intonation, and dramatic look, I felt she had a "Marilyn air." But we couldn't seem to locate her at the time. So after an extensive search, we went with Eloise Laws, sister of Jazz artist Hubert Laws. She wound up in the group for about a minute. Flip Wilson's girlfriend at the time, when Eloise didn't show up for rehearsal one day, her excuse seemed, if you'll excuse the pun, rather flippant. "My boyfriend didn't want me to attend."

I shot back, "Well, Flip has nothing to do with it!"

Florence tartly added, "Nor your lackluster appearance with us on *The Tonight Show,*" about Miss Laws's lack of "background duty" smile on Florence's lead, "Magic in My Life."

That's when we went right back to Broadway to find the mighty Marjorie Barnes for the Marilyn position. It's where we had already found the affable Danny Miller Beard as Billy's replacement. I used to tease Danny that he was the only Black cat I knew who dug the recording of "Stoned Soul Picnic." The new two added a jolt of energy to the group, but soon both Danny and Marjorie had other ambitions—it seemed The 5th Dimension would become a stop on the road—a training ground of sorts—for our varied replacements' creative goals, fueling their artistic freedom, so to speak. We took it in stride, and in the process, we worked with some refreshing talent. My all-time favorite who I brought in the group, a former *Soul Train* dancer with extensive recording experience—and our youngest member ever—was the striking Joyce Wright (Pierce). Like a sister to me, and a fellow Virgo, her dynamic range added pizzazz to our act, yet Joyce always had the utmost respect in approaching our legendary tunes. Michael Procter joined in the Billy position, and this incarnation in the late seventies through the early eighties—Florence, Ron, Joyce, Michael, and myself—was a winner as we scored back big in Vegas and appeared once again at the White House. A woman of faith, when Joyce wanted to leave to marry and start a family, I understood, but over the years, I wished she had never departed. Michael, although a charismatic asset, was the only person I ever got nose to nose with in a near altercation. Let's just say his ego issue, like demanding the group be called "Michael Procter and The 5th Dimension" wasn't going to happen!

Along the way, The 5th Dimension members included Michele "Mic" Bell, who later was nominated for a Tony for the Broadway revival of *Showboat*, Eugene Barry-Hill, the current star of the Tony-winning Broadway sensation *Kinky Boots*, the Soul singer Lou Courtney, the powerful Greg Walker, formerly of Santana, the splendid Jamila Ajibade, the lead of the Broadway touring company of *Aida*, and the personable Van Jewell, who was also in The Friends of Distinction. Jazz chanteuse Phyllis Battle was with us for many years, a nice lady whose efforts I appreciated along with all of the other first-class artists who helped The 5th Dimension legacy to prevail in contemporary yet familiar ways. And may I gladly add, today Miss Florence LaRue timelessly leads The 5th Dimension along with gentlemen of song Willie Williams, Leonard Tucker, and Floyd Smith (the latter who's taken my slot in the bass position). Gospel singer Patrice Morris adds to the quintet's solid sound and warm fellowship. Yes, The 5th Dimension is forever beloved and continues to play to sold-out crowds everywhere.

I told you about my father, Herman, leaving Mama June a note when we were all babies—that he essentially couldn't hang no more. Did he want his freedom? But at what price? One night, years later, I had finished a show in LA with The Hi-Fi's, and this nice-looking middle-aged man came up to me and said, "I loved your show," with all the usual pleasantries. And then he added, "I'm your father." Just like that. As my jaw dropped, I looked at him more closely and could almost see the resemblance to me, but more to my brother, Duck. He continued, "I am very sorry. You don't even have to speak to me or anything." He just tracked me down; how he found me, I don't know. He handed me a folded piece of paper, mumbling a contrite, "Well, here's my address if you ever want to keep in touch." And he walked off, as was his style. Everyone around, seeing the color drained from my face, started asking, "God, man, what just happened?" I couldn't say nothing. I just couldn't believe it. And I couldn't tell Mama June because, boy…

Near the dawning of the new year, 1991, the savvy management team of Sterling-Winters came up with the idea of reuniting The 5th Dimension, "The Original 5th Dimension," as we were going to be billed. And Donald Trump was only too accommodating to offer his majestic Trump Plaza in Atlantic City as our initial venue. We were quickly all in, thanks to the schedule-coordinating efforts of our managers, but more so because each of us wanted to be together for old times' sake, although we were far from an "Oldies" act!

When Marilyn and Billy met Florence, Ron, and me for rehearsal, naturally the first tune we attempted was "Up-Up and Away." And it was like no time had passed, like we had just been on vacation. However, the song took on new meaning, as we had all grown as artists and as people; yes, we were freer than ever. We even changed a line in our Jimmy Webb-penned signature tune by one word: "Love is waiting there (in my beautiful balloon)" became "*The* love is waiting there…" We wanted to acknowledge God's amazing grace. In fact, some young group in the rehearsal room next to us thought we were an entirely new act; they later winked at us in the elevator, calling us "fresh!"

Our opening night on December 29, 1990, was electric. The crowd was wild with anticipation before we even hit the stage. With the announcement, "Please welcome for the first time in fifteen years, The Original 5th Dimension!" the roar from the audience became deafening. Our reunion cavalcade, with musical staging and choreography by Arthur Faria, who not only worked so masterfully with us on *Ain't Misbehavin'* but with Lena Horne for her award-winning *The Lady and Her Music* on Broadway, defined "sizzling." I'll never forget not only our singing the greatest hits to standing ovations, but bombastic showstoppers like Ronald's lead on "MacArthur Park," the complete version with all the intricate, syncopated backups. Or Florence stepping forward with a spellbinding "Never My Love," a song Marilyn originally soloed on. Billy's "The Worst that Could Happen," into Marilyn's "Wedding Bell Blues," complete with their patented "cat and mouse" skit, drew oohs and ahs, and my own tasty trip with "The 5th Dimension Rap" was something cool, out of the blue. But I admit to getting choked up as we punctuated a swinging version of Sinatra's "Where or When" with "Reunited (and it feels so good)."

We toured with that special "Original" reunion show to rave reviews for a limited number of years while Marilyn and Billy continued their duet and solo careers simultaneously, and Florence, Ronald, and I performed with the current version of The 5th Dimension as well. During this time, The Original 5th Dimension appeared on the top-rated *The Arsenio Hall Show* right before receiving our star on the Hollywood Walk of Fame. Surprisingly, my father attended the ceremony. And of course, Mama June was there, and that was the first time she had seen him, her ex-husband, in forty years. I kept thinking, "Whoa, now this parental 'reunion' is kinda deep," while trying to get my star with the reunited group.

Then somebody announced, "Hey, we're gonna have a reception afterward." And my father was standing close and asked like an innocent kid, "Oh, a reception? Where is it?" Well, a simmering Mama June was standing nearby, too, and she walked right up to him and proclaimed in her deepest tone, "If you come, I'm kicking your ass!" At the time, my father was kind of paralyzed due to a minor stroke and wasn't too strong. He looked at his former wife, a church lady, mind you, with all those years of frustration built up, now appearing like a house on fire. And he didn't come to our party, neither.

I loved my father, but I didn't like him for what he did to my mother. As you can see, we kept in contact; Mama June didn't understand or approve, but she didn't stop us. One day my father's current wife called. "If you guys could just come by and see him," when he initially had his stroke. He was driving when it came upon him, and he hit a tree, too. So there we were at his hospital bedside, Duck, my sisters Joanie and Merilyn, and I. My father had lost most of his speech at that point and kept attempting to say something. My stepmother looked at me. "He's trying to tell you he likes your watch, LaMonte. He thinks it's beautiful." I took it off right away and instinctively placed it on his left wrist, the side he was paralyzed on. And his hand jumped. Later, his doctor told him the prognosis had improved, that he would use his left hand again. I'd like to think the watch brought back the feeling in that hand. Recently, a friend pointed out that symbolically, I was giving my father back the time we lost, forgiving him for his irresponsibility in leaving us. "Yep, yep, yep," is all I can summon to such profundity. I never had anything against my father; I believe people do what they have to do—you know, "go where they wanna go." He made his decision and had to live with it. That's why when I grew up and could do anything, I made my own decision to always take care of Mama June. But in giving my father my watch, we both found a new sense of freedom.

In the early nineties, when The current 5th Dimension was appearing on cruise lines, we flew to Saint Thomas to board the ship and got caught up in the disastrous Hurricane Marilyn. The 150-mile-per-hour winds blew the entire roof off the hotel where we were staying before embarking. As our suites, situated on the second floor, became highly vulnerable, a quick-witted Florence ran into the bathroom with Bible in hand and remained protected in the tub for six hours. The guys, Ron, Greg, and I were all in one room, frightened for our lives as the devastation occurring outside became ear-splitting. We wondered frequently if Florence was in danger while we remained separated. And we prayed.

When we finally found one another, she breathlessly explained that while retreating to safety, her room's ceiling had fallen in, with debris and glass landing in the center of the bed! Thank God Florence was OK, but the hurricane's aftermath left us with no water available but a trickling fountain outside. It made for my three-hour, impossible-to-get-the-lather-out shampoo session one night! When the hotel's rationed food had run its course, we all took a trek to a nearby mall and did some "creative looting." Crawling through a broken window, I grabbed what I could, getting my hands on artichokes and okra. "It's Hobo Flats time," I thought. "Making something out of nearly nothing!"

Since the airport was torn up, the army was sent in to construct a makeshift runway. Every day there was a lottery, and when our names came up, we stranded Americans at the island's hotels got the chance to get out on a small transport plane. When it was my turn, I never saw so much Gucci luggage being discarded in my life, thrown overboard as we were strapped in that l'il ole plane like paratroopers. No one dared risk weighing us down! Also keeping it "light" was one celebratory young couple who got married on the runway before we flew off. It led us to Puerto Rico, where the Red Cross greeted us with Kentucky Fried Chicken before we caught our connecting flights. Now, if you think this entire tale will lead to one of my analogies about sweet freedom, you're mistaken. I just wanted to tell you that was the best damn chicken I've ever tasted in my life! And yes, I was extremely thankful.

Somewhere in the late eighties, The 5th Dimension was working nonstop, like three years straight without a single vacation. Our manager, Jason Winters, kept promising us one, but it never seemed to materialize. I finally had enough and did something I've never done in my over four decades with the group; I had a former member step in for me as I got my freedom in the blue seas of Rio de Janeiro. Running down the beach's glistening sands, I didn't notice that nobody else was out swimming as I went to frolic in the fifteen-foot waves. All the UDT (Underwater Demolition Team) training my navy days taught me couldn't save me from getting caught in the undertow while attempting to ride those big boys in. I was getting pulled out to sea farther and farther, and after trying to ride a third wave, my energy was all but spent. A crowd had gathered on the shore because I was in deep trouble. Somehow, as I dug into the wet sand in one final, feeble attempt at self-preservation, a man reached out and grabbed me. It wasn't the hand of God, but maybe. I didn't notice as I staggered to dry land that my trunks were down to my knees—a "wardrobe malfunction" unbecoming a member of The 5th Dimension—or that I was clutching my hotel-room key. I guess through it all, my survival mode dictated I wasn't going to have to pay for a new key! I lay on the beach for about three hours until I regained my strength. Drifting in and out of sleep, I realized my near death experience was a wake-up call, not about how playing hooky can go awry, but about what is and isn't important in life. That's why I always say, "If I wake up each day, I'm happy." Now isn't that the ultimate freedom!

CHAPTER 8

CEASE FIRE

"Dig two graves for all revenge..."

One day not too long ago, a new song came to me. Like all the photos of women and the wonders of the world "I take on one take," it came about because, as I told one interviewer, "I just see things." Yep, with writing a song, it's the same instantaneous process as my being inspired to snap a shot; maybe I just feel things when it comes to words and putting them to music. It happened with "A Love Like Ours," and it occurred again with "Cease Fire." Now this song was intended to start with a spoken verse. I guess I wanted to leave the poetry as is to underscore from the beginning the mood of this being a sort of grown-up nursery rhyme.

There is a weapon of mass destruction
and it's easy to find
just look in the mirror
because it's us, mankind...

Then the music swells, if you can imagine, in the genre of Michael Jackson's "Earth Song," but I'd like to continue presenting my song, excerpted for you here, as poetry.

Cease fire,
say it loud enough
Cease fire
can't say it often enough
Just two words, "cease fire," can mean so much
two words can bring wars to a halt
who's to blame, when we're all at fault.

No one was born with a gun in hand
so what happens when we become woman and man
without greed and prejudice we were born
but it's the reason so many lives are torn
there's a fate for hate, and it's not heaven's gate
that's the message, let's get that straight
words can hurt as much as any wound
but God's Word can lift spirits to the moon.
Cease fire, lay your weapons down

——

Remember, dig two graves for all revenge
Cease fire,
Cease fire,
Amen, Amen
(copyright 2012, LaMonte McLemore)

The line "dig two graves for all revenge," may confound some, but it comes from what my Grandma taught me when I was a twelve-year-old boy. Once again, I was singled out among my brother and sisters, this time to hear the following true tale of tales, one I believe was intended to change the entire course of my life.

Here's the backstory. My grandfather, Lucius Shaver, first encountered Grandma in Oklahoma, when she was in her late teens. As he took in the sight of this touchingly sad but far from woebegotten, astonishingly radiant Native American maiden sitting on the side of the train tracks, Grandpa's attraction to Gertrude Whiteside was instantaneous. I guess that "instant thing" runs in the family! You see, Grandpa was working there for the railroad. In actuality, its further expansion would bring the destruction of Grandma's entire village, leaving her with no place to live. Amid such a moral dilemma, Grandpa would share his sandwich at lunch break with the object of his affection. Day after day, he talked to the reserved yet wise young woman who responded with a knowing look in her wistful yet hopeful eyes, while speaking in a broken type of English, revealing her Cherokee ancestry. Upon completing the job at hand, Lucius needed no summoning of courage to ask if she would accompany him back to Black Rock, Arkansas, to have his hand in marriage. Gertrude's reply was equally strong, "Yes, but only if my brother comes with me." And that he did.

Now here's where Grandma led into the most sultry part of the story. Standing over six feet tall, with muscles for miles, her brother had flowing onyx locks that cascaded over his broad shoulders. The white women of Black Rock would literally gush over this bronze specimen of masculinity who appeared to come right out of a Hollywood "cowboys and Indians" movie. The vision of the entranced ladies stroking his taut, tawny physique and running their hands through his sometimes braided tresses, must have set the prejudiced townsmen into a frenzy. Until one day, when they decided enough was enough.

Grandma proceeded to end the unforgettable scenario in hushed tones. While taking a walk, she came upon her beloved brother. He was tied to a tree. As his body hung lifelessly, she witnessed he had been tarred and feathered, too. The young man had been lynched.

I sat there misty-eyed, mouth agape as Grandma carefully went on, gaining more vocal strength. "LaMonte, I do not tell you this story for you to hate anybody." Then she seemingly chanted to me in her unruffled, measured fashion, "LaMonte, whenever you seek revenge, you dig two graves...one for the offender, one for yourself." And then she disclosed her nearly immediate release from such a nightmare with a phrase that has become permanently etched in my mind:

"If God can forgive, who are we not to?"

I responded, not yet realizing the full impact of her mantra, "But, Grandma, how horrible. Weren't you angry?"

"Of course, I broke down in tears, and people gathered to help. But what could I do? Even the police were on the side of the Ku Klux Klan," she answered rapidly, still retaining her poise. There was nobody to march for Civil Rights then. As well, Grandma barely knew English at the time, but as I recall, somewhere in her early life missionaries had inspired her. Yes, my grandma found her Grace in an instantaneous manner—that running concept in my familial history does not escape me. She rose to her spiritual plane, trusting in the highest power of all to forgive that easily. "Whenever you seek revenge, you dig two graves." She meant to let things go, because revenge is part of the cycle of hate, and if you're looking for it, who knows the fate? There's no guarantee you'll come back from it. Cease fire, because you're turning the fire on yourself. Revenge is nothing else but revenge. What do you really gain from it? Later, when Grandpa passed and Grandma decided to move to St. Louis where her children, including my mother, had settled, she continued her journey by taking care of my family. It was on her own path that my grandma set me free on the adventurously happy, unconditionally forgiving theme of my life's trajectory.

Recently a lovely woman from the Smithsonian came to visit me to pick up one of The 5th Dimension's famous, designer costumes that was a hallmark of our image. From trendsetting Native American-inspired outfits to "Moon Babies" (as our designer dubbed our gossamer blue and silver duds), we covered it all, and I was glad to have that aspect of our persona acknowledged. As thanks, I even demonstrated some of my culinary skills as the lady from our most heralded institute casually interviewed me. She asked what my secret was, referring to not only the joyfulness The 5th stood for, but how I continue to carry it on personally in my daily routine.

I responded, alluding to what I already said in the last chapter, "If I wake up each morning on this side of the dirt, I'm successful!"

She requested I go on, so I explained, "If I make someone smile, if I make someone laugh, then I'm really successful!"

Friends often say, "Mac, I call telling you I'm literally dying, and by the time I'm ready to hang up, you have me crying…with laughter!"

Grandma would say, "People go around worrying about what they want, when more important is what they need." Our health, our family, our house, our food is all that really matters. There are no failures. In all we try, we challenge ourselves to honor our God. And thus, why should anything—or anyone, for that matter—ever bother us? How important is it really? Even Mother Teresa is quoted as saying, "In the final analysis, it is between you and God. It was never between you and them anyway." Every day, I can still hear Grandma say in her special way, "Who are we to judge?"

So, how am I gonna close a chapter such as this? But of course, with a touch of humor! Around 1969, as a member of The 5th Dimension, I was invited to be a contestant on TV's naughty-but-nice game show, *The*

Dating Game. One of the producers, who was a friend of mine, knew how crazy I could be and told the show's execs, "That zany LaMonte should write his own questions!" for my interview of the three "bachelorettes" who appeared behind the partition, one who I'd choose as my date. So I mischievously came up with, "Since I'd like your phone number, but you can't give it to me on TV, can you just 'breathe' it to me?"

Well, each of them answered in a Morse code of oohs, ahs, moans, and soft-core mayhem that should have gotten the broadcast a scolding from the censors. But note that before all the frivolities, I posed to my friend the producer, who happened to be African American, "Why are Black contestants relegated to choosing solely Black dates on your show? That's not the way today's world is going…or mine. You're in a position to inquire with the powers that be and stand up for diversity." Well, that producer did stand up…and was later fired. I'll never really know why, and I certainly appeared on the show with three enchanting African American young women as my potential dates, but I'd like to think my inquiry at least planted a seed for the interracial change we'd later see on that show and many others.

Now, are you still laughing…thinking…trying to voice what your phone number would sound like by breathing it? You know what—it's all cool. Now, won't you join me in a chorus of

> *Cease fire, say it loud enough,*
> *Cease fire, can't say it often enough…*

CHAPTER 9

A LOVE LIKE OURS

"Wanting to be together, yet wanting to be free..."

I think there's been a misconception about me, in that my image back in the day was perceived as that of a global playboy. When asked who my favorite types of ladies were, I'm sure my glib response, "Two kinds: foreign and domestic!" to people like Don Cornelius on *Soul Train*, contributed to the misunderstanding. Then there was that moment during the TV special, "Burt Bacharach in Shangri-La" when Burt asked if any of The 5th Dimension's members played instruments. I piped up after Marilyn and Florence's respectable and respective "piano" and "violin" nods, "I play the field!" Sweets was quick to chortle, "And he's not kidding!" And how on earth could our chaste original fan-club newsletter state that my favorite sports were "broad jumping and breast stroking?"

I laughed at the myth not only because I was enjoying life, but because "the real LaMonte" had a deep-seated respect for women. I don't need to remind you that I was essentially raised by Grandma and Mama June and had two sisters. It's why in my work as a photographer, I never used my position to take advantage of women. In fact, one model wondered if I might be gay because I didn't make a pass at her. I simply felt and still feel that business is business, especially when it comes to having the privilege of illuminating the heart and soul, as well as the mystery of women. To this day, I'll receive messages on Facebook from models I've portrayed who I haven't seen in years; the experience seemed to be life-altering for them. To capture a woman's truth in a split second of mutual revelation is indeed a gift.

Just like I gave a little love letter to you about my favorite (and not so!) tunes from The 5th Dimension songbook, may I present a chronological love letter to the important women in my life? They, too, were gifts, some obvious, some who brought about a lesson learned, all of whom I am fortunate to have known.

My mother never talked about sex—teaching us about pregnancy—so I never knew anything about that side of it when I was very young. Mama June was not only bashful but busy; she just didn't have the time to tell us. Even Grandma, who was always home with us, never told us about sex, so we had to kind of learn on our own. Finally, Mama June's sister, we'd call her Aunt Ceal, offered, should we have any questions of an intimate nature. But my earliest recollection about sex has to do with when Little Johnny, the perennial bad kid of the 'hood, came by, and we shared this exchange:

"Whatcha doing, LaMonte?"

"I'm just listening to the radio." (Note: TV wasn't around then!)

"Well, then, let's go to Mary's house."

"What are we going down there for, Johnny?"

"We're gonna get some pussy."

I replied, "OK, let me get my coat and stuff," happy as a lark but having zero idea what he was talking about.

As Mama June saw me getting ready to leave, she asked, "Where are you going, son?"

"I'm going with Johnny, going to this little girl's house in the neighborhood."

"Going down there for what, LaMonte?"

"Going down there to get some pussy."

And with that, I got smacked upside my head so fast, I figured whatever pussy was, I didn't want no part of it…I just wanted to live my little life as a kid, playing ball and whatever other games we could play for nothing, because we didn't have nothing! So I never really thought about girls that much, when toward the end of grade school—I must have been twelve—I had my first heartthrob, this little girl named Barbara. I just liked her, I don't know why. She was too cute and plain nice. For instance, I always had jam sandwiches, as in two pieces of bread jammed together, and some peanut butter if I got lucky. We were sitting in the schoolyard at lunchtime, and Barbara knew I had these simple sandwiches and said coyly, "Oh, I love peanut butter, LaMonte, would you like my chicken sandwich?"

"Oh, really? You sure?" I'd blush, and she would angelically hand it over. In all the classrooms, they'd either seat me in front or in back of her because the whole school knew there was this puppy love going on. And it wasn't even about first love. It wasn't about nothin', I just liked her as a person…and certainly no sex, because remember, I didn't wanna think about that. One day I came to school, and I noticed Barbara wasn't there, and everyone was looking at me kinda funny. "I thought I was clean. I might be a little raggedy," I joshed. And the teacher said in the most somber of tones, "LaMonte, I have something to tell you. Barbara was in the car with her father. There was an accident, and she got killed." And that was really it for me. Even to this day, I weep for that innocent time and the memory of that precious little girl.

Fortunately another aunt, known as "Big Sis," lived in a relatively better neighborhood. Sensing my sadness over such a loss, she said, "Come stay with us. It'll get you out of the ghetto area, and you'll get to use our address for placement in a better school."

"That's great," I thought aloud, "because Big Sis has an indoor toilet!" At this supposed step-up in education, Big Blondelle, who looked just like, well, Big Blondelle, was greedily taking the virginity away from all the junior-high-school males. She'd just take advantage of them in a most aggressive fashion. I wasn't really interested or impressed when all the boys would come back and boast, "Hey, I just had sex with Big Blondelle," in a nearby garage or whatever. Because I was elusive, one day while I was sitting next to her in English class, I became Blondelle's target. She opened her legs and demanded, "LaMonte, look here!" and I witnessed the ugliest thing I'd ever seen. I responded, "Don't do that no more!"

She baited me. "Why?" and opened her legs even farther. I reached down between her thighs—don't ask me why—and she clamped those big ole fat things like a vise. I couldn't remove my hand as she raised hers with a smirk, "Mr. Johnson, LaMonte's got his hand up under my dress!"

"Mr. McLemore, how could you! You must get a note from your parents, and don't come back to school until you do!" was my admonishment. I wasn't about to tell Mama June where I'd had my hand, so I had one of my friends forge a note of the requisite disappointment and regret. When I got back to school, Big Blondelle stood in the hallway boisterously laughing as the guys greeted me with "Hey, Mac, what's happening?" When I went to shake their hands, they backed off. "Not that hand, brother!"

After that trauma, I took out a couple of girls for casual dates, and then I met Gail, my first true love, at the end of senior year. In fact, I was ready to come out of high school, and she was ready to go in. Gail represented a pivotal chapter of my life. It wasn't even a sexual attraction at first, it was just a mad crush. I thought she was the prettiest thing I'd ever seen besides little Barbara. Come to think of it, they almost looked similar with their long silky hair.

> *Looked like coffee with the right amount of cream,*
> *Carnation baby, that turned into a dream.*

Shut up! (That's actually the lyric from one of my early songwriting forays.) So naturally I wanted to take Gail to the movies. "You'll have to meet my parents, you know. They're both teachers," she cautioned, a bit full of herself. I was scared to death to meet and have to impress such high-class folks. Her father began his inquisition. "Young man, what are your plans for the future?"

"I'd like to be a baseball player."

"Well, I don't want my daughter involved with anybody in the sports field…you don't have any other goals?"

"I'd like to be a photog—"

"Shootin' all those nude pictures. Nah, nah," he bellowed suspiciously, like he had seen one too many himself.

"What about singing, sir?"

"Hell no!" he yelped, unlike any teacher I knew.

It sure seemed Grandma's sensible three-things rule struck out in this household. Consequently, we had to sneak and date. She'd go to the movies with her girlfriends, I'd start out with the guys, and we'd meet. As my story goes, it became necessary that I join the navy. I will genuinely state, despite all my problems there, from my trying to be their photographer to my run-in with a redneck, that the thing that got me through my military misery—besides my brother Duck's madcap visit—was the heart-melting thought of Gail. Rather, a matter of the naïve heart kept me going. I was soon to discover when I got out of the service and wound up in Los Angeles, where Gail ironically had moved, that our reunion would be anything but "kismet."

I immediately went to Gail's home, where her mom covered with "Gail is busy right now." I could tell some guy was there, so I thought, "OK, I mean, I've been gone." A night later, I went to see a friend of mine from St. Louis days. Interestingly, his name was Cherry. Duck was with me and noticed Gail's car outside. I felt a twinge as I said casually, "Let me stop up and holla at Cherry." Someone departing the apartment building let us in without our having to get buzzed up. As I started to knock, I halted at the muffled sound of these sexy cries and oohs and ahs coming through Cherry's door. Then I froze at the thought of what was going on. "Whatcha gonna do, LaMonte?" Duck said with concerned anticipation after offering his flashlight, which I proceeded to drop.

The resounding thud brought Cherry to the door. "Uh hey, whatcha doing, man," a startled Cherry sputtered.

"I just came to say hi," I said, nonplussed.

"Oh yeah? Good. I'll see ya later."

"Can I have a drink of water?" Duck interjected with cloaked mischief.

"You don't need no water." Cherry was not amused as Duck simply pushed the door open, and I went in. Before me was a fold-down bed, clothes, undergarments…everything, with Gail, I quickly surmised, hiding behind the wall. So Cherry went to the refrigerator and came back with a ticked off, "Here's your ice water," and Duck looked at me like, "Man, you ain't gonna' kick his butt…and hers?"

But I proclaimed, "Come on, let's just go!" And we did. I was numb. Here was the one woman I was waiting for; she was gonna be my first. I was devastated. All the stories I'd been hearing about Gail, the ones I didn't want to believe—from her sister, no less—that I filtered out, came back at me as I found myself calling Gail a few hours later. "How you doin', Gail?"

"Oh, I'm tired from a long day at school."

"Oh yeah, some school all right," I said bitterly as a torrent of accusations spilled out. "Look, I not only witnessed what was happening at Cherry's tonight, but I heard from your sister about multiple pregnancies, abortions…I know everything!" My tidal wave was met with what seemed like an eternity of silence, until one of Gail's girlfriends got on the line. I figured Gail must have called her over for consolation when she got home from Cherry's. Her girlfriend howled, "What did you say to Gail? She's so upset…wait, she's trying to cut her wrists! Hang up, hang up!" In disgust, I threw the receiver on the floor. It bounced in what appeared to be slow motion and landed perfectly on the hook. It freaked me out, because I certainly had no intention of doing so. Since they wouldn't have been able to readily call out for help with what was known as an open line, the intervening hand of God saved Gail's life.

I started drinking rum and Cokes, and I'm not a drinker. I got in my car and just drove and drove. It was dangerous; I was light-headed, I didn't know how fast I was going, and I didn't know where I was going. I looked up, and I was at the Mexican border, from Los Angeles to Tijuana in one blind, extended whoosh. So I parked my car and walked down a long street of assorted nightclubs, where tourists, sailors, and Mexicans were hanging out.

A guy stepped forward. "Hey, you want to have my *see-ster* for sex?" With such crassness compounding my pain, I hauled off and hit him hard enough to knock him out. Good thing I played ball and was in peak shape, because when the guy came to, relatively quickly, I wound up with ten Mexican cats chasing me. I jumped over a fence; a menacing dog was there, and I inadvertently stepped on its head. I kept going. Eventually, nine of them stopped running. They just got tired, except one who was unrelenting. I turned around, looked him dead in the eye, and said, "C'mon!" When he realized the other nine were long gone, that sucker started running back the other way. "Shit, what am I gonna do?" I sighed, knowing I couldn't get my car, as it was parked down the street from where I punched the guy. I needed to keep on walking. As I approached a little shack, an elfin boy appeared and whispered, "Here!" He grabbed my hand with a "Come, come," and led me farther into the Mexican mirage, which then manifested into a house of ill repute. The prostitute there started undressing me, and I was so out of it, so messed up in the head, so broken in spirit, that I went with it. I thought, "If somebody's gonna be first, I don't wanna know who it is." I wouldn't even look at the woman's face. And that was my first sexual experience, a dazed and dispassionate one, at all of twenty-one, fresh out of the navy in '56. In the sobering light of day, disappointed in myself and my reaction to Gail's misdoings, I fearfully found my car with (luckily) none of my Mexican chasers surrounding it. I drove out of Tijuana as fast as I could, knowing in my gut I'd be focusing my energies on baseball and photography for many years to come.

Now, Deedee illustrated a totally different chapter. She painted a picture of refreshing, down-to-earth chic. A classically poised, Dorothy Dandridge type, she was a model with singing aspirations. I stopped by one Sunday to see her sister, Janis, who was otherwise occupied and wound up taking Deedee out for some ice cream. We ended up dating for eight years, throughout the late sixties and early seventies, with only one major argument about something so silly that my lips are sealed on that one! We even appeared on an afternoon game show together as a promising couple among the married members of The 5th Dimension with their spouses—Marilyn and Billy, Ron and his cherished Bobette, and Florence, who was wed by that time to our manager, Marc. Deedee and I effortlessly fit that breezy TV bill of fare, because we were just so easygoing together. In fact, everyone who met Deedee liked her, so I wasn't surprised when a captivated Harry Belafonte just happened to call and say hi while I was at her apartment. She met Harry backstage at one of his shows I took her and her mother to, and I didn't realize it at the moment, that he smoothly got her number. But that was OK because conversely, Deedee saw me out one night at a club with Ulla, a German stewardess I happened to meet through Frank Sinatra. When our eyes met, I simply went over and asked Deedee to dance. She smiled, and we did. The lady was just cool like that.

We're still friends; in fact, my wife and I attended a Thanksgiving party Deedee and her husband, Carl, recently gave. He's a great guy, someone who I not-so-jokingly told I would shoot if he ever treated Deedee badly. You see, they were married at my house, to be specific. My friends are my friends, and with someone like Deedee, friendship is an absolute treasure. At first my wife was reluctant to connect with one of my ex-girlfriends, but she and Deedee hit it off immediately. Both woman are remarkable in their own classy ways…and secure.

I just alluded to Ulla, and it in no way was meant to indicate our time together was fleeting. She too was an important part of my life. A gentle, nature-loving soul who had a caring way about the world at large, it was fitting that this tall, dark-haired lovely traveled the globe as a flight attendant but always made everyone feel at home in her presence. One night while waiting for a cab outside the Americana ballroom, where The 5th Dimension was performing, we were accosted by some rather rude remarks about our interracial status. Even in Manhattan, things were not so progressive in 1968, but Ulla was. She reacted by grabbing my arm protectively, then she emphatically asked to come back inside to my hotel room, not for a romantic liaison, mind you, but to sincerely get to know me better. We talked way into the morning hours. It was her compassion that ignited my passion. Now her dad was another trip, especially when Ulla informed him she was seeing a man of color. "What damn color? Don't bring him around here," he blustered, but I'll refrain from calling him an out-and-out Nazi, especially because as fate would have it, even he was a fan of The 5th Dimension. In fact he had a crush on Marilyn! So we met up, and what can I say, yet again The 5th Dimension done brought folk together! As we chatted and joked, the transformation of this traditional man of German decent was quite moving, especially since Mama June herself was color blind. She welcomed a visiting Ulla at her St. Louis door with open arms and a "You poor skinny little thing. Come on in and let me fatten you up," for good measure. Ulla decided to move in with me to be closer, but because of the group's touring schedule and her own "flight pattern," it turned out she saw less of me as a roommate than when we lived separately. We parted as friends to the end, her heart of gold being the memorable quality that most of the ladies of my life have in common.

The pleasing thought of Jayne Kennedy, that iconic beauty of seventies pop culture and my dear friend, brings a sigh of joy, always and forever. Our initial encounter is something Jayne still teases me about. The 5th Dimension was working at the Hollywood Bowl, and as custom had it, we'd all go out into the audience during the "Let the Sunshine In" component of our "Aquarius" finale to bring fans up on stage to dance with us. I had already seen this stunning girl from the footlights, so I made a beeline to reach for who turned out to be Jayne. However, another girl suddenly reached up, saying "I'll go!" and kept hold so tight that I couldn't say, "No, I wanted the other girl!" The female with the strong-arm tactic wound up being quite the spectacle, bowing and throwing kisses on stage after our dance. As circumstances would nicely have it, after the show, Jayne and her husband, the actor Leon Isaac Kennedy, came backstage, so I thought, "Well, she's with someone, but at least I get a chance to meet her." With her doe-eyed demeanor, she introduced herself. "Hi, LaMonte, I'm Jayne, and that's the first time I've ever been turned down for a transvestite." Turns out the girl with the grip was the biggest female impersonator in California! Jayne, however, was the real deal, so I artfully requested, "Do you model?" She demurred. "Well, I just came from Cleveland—" but her husband pitched in, "Are you kidding? Of course she does!"

So I made the photographic appointment, she came to my studio, and Jayne eventually ended up being my first million-dollar model, and one without an ounce of attitude. If I called her at 2:00 a.m. and told her we needed to shoot pictures in a few hours with an 8:00 a.m. call time, she'd enthusiastically inquire, "What clothes should I bring?" while other models would complain. I predicted, "Jayne, one day you're gonna be up on a billboard." She'd respond, "You have more confidence in me than I have."

Of course, she not only wound up on billboards across America but became the country's premiere female sportscaster, a first for both women and African Americans—Mohammad Ali wouldn't have interviews with anybody but Jayne. This happily reminds me of another of my impressive models, Kathleen Bradley, who became the first African American woman to join ranks with "Barker's Beauties," as featured on the popular game show, *The Price Is Right*.

But back to Jayne, what a team we were! Anywhere I'd send her early on, she'd get the job. Against her initial doubts, she wound up being part of *The Dean Martin Show*'s merry troop of sexy backup singer-dancers known as The Ding-a-Lings. "Jayne, Dean is having auditions for his TV show!" I'd begin to cheer her on. "Oh, I can't dance," she'd respond meekly. I'd keep pushing. "Just go down there, because once they see you, they'll find something for you to do!" Well, she arrived timidly late, but for Jane, auditions were anything but over; the casting director took one look at her, and she got the job. "But I can't sing." Jayne pouted. The response was, "That's fine, we'll just send you for singing lessons and dance classes." That's how magnetic she was.

Then there was the time Bob Hope was adding new models to his famous USO tours to entertain the troops of the armed forces. "Oh, I was only one of the semifinalists in the Miss USA Pageant, he'd want a first-place winner." Jayne truly believed this. "Just let him see ya!" I said like a baseball coach and drove her down to the go-see. As Jayne exited my car, Mr. Hope was passing by with his assistant and observed in his stage voice, "Now that's the caliber of girl I want with me!" And of course, Jayne was booked on the patriotic world tour of top entertainment.

I was dating a girl then, and Jayne was married, but there was such combustible energy between Jayne and me, not only in our collaborations but with our intoxicating personal chemistry, that up to that time I'd never felt anything like that for anybody. I mean, I'd never used the word "love" with girls I was dating because that word was too special, and I wanted to be sure, but with Jayne, if we'd even had a chance to be together, I probably would have said the word love. That's how close we were. I had reconciled myself to the fact that at least I was fortunate enough to be her friend when Jayne was the object of every red-blooded guy's fantasy. But to my surprise, even my girlfriend compassionately mused, "Too bad Jayne is married, because I'd like you guys to have a chance." And then, when Jayne got divorced, Leon stated, "Jayne, if you get together with anyone after me, it should be LaMonte." But she began seeing a good guy, Bill Overton, and they ended up marrying. I was involved with someone new, too, so we inevitably wound up friends for life. Oh, but that electricity between us, we continue to laugh about it to this day!

One time The 5th Dimension was getting off the tour bus to perform outside of San Francisco, and this family with two young girls came up for an autograph. So of course I went right over to them. "You're so sweet, how old are you?" I asked one of the two little cuties, who proudly pronounced she was eight. "Ten more years, come back and see me," I said, without a trace of lasciviousness, in admiration of her innocent prettiness. Cut to a decade later, we're rehearsing *Ain't Misbehavin'* at the Fairmont in San Francisco, and I receive a call. "Is this LaMonte? You signed an autograph for me when I was a child, and told me to come back in ten years. Well, I'm eighteen now…and I'm back!" I had no idea who the honeyed voice on the other end of the line belonged to. Busy working with the show's choreographer but with my curiosity stirred, I told her to meet me in the lobby in a bit.

Upon my arrival, there waiting was an espresso-maned, multiethnic, languid beauty. "Hi, my name is Lisa," she said displaying the autograph. I was flashing back to our initial meeting and thinking she had turned out just as I'd envisioned. "Are you still a photographer? I'd like you to do my portfolio," she cooed.

"Yeah, I'd be glad to," I responded, thinking what a story this was. So I invited Lisa and her family to our show and at curtain call, I stepped forward and said, "I don't usually do this, but ten years ago, I told this young fan to come back…and she just showed up not only with the autograph I gave her, but holding the same little dress she was wearing at the time!" As the spotlight hit her waving the dress, the audience collectively oohed.

I proceeded to shoot her portfolio, and we hit it off but didn't formally date, as I was seeing this delightful Korean girl, Renie, who had a story all her own. But at that point, it was good to be friends with Lisa, especially knowing our own interesting backstory. In fact, I got her a T-shirt that said, "It pays."

"Huh?" Lisa asked of such a logo.

"It pays to be kind to children!" I retorted. From then on, everyone would call out to her with "Hey, Pays!"

May I take a sidebar to tell you about Renie? For it's her indomitable spirit that deserves a salute, if not a movie about her life. How I met her had to do with this guy coming by saying there was a girl he wanted me to do modeling shots for, but I could tell, knowing of his questionable character, he didn't mean this poor girl much good. So every time I learned he'd be taking her out, I'd make a photo shoot appointment for her. We also wound up hitting it off. We didn't really date or nothing, but one time at Christmas, since we both didn't have plans, we agreed we should go out. Just as I stopped by her apartment, her supposed boyfriend drove up unannounced, and I squarely said, "Well, it's up to you, Renie." And she got into my car. So I figured we were tight but never thought our ride would result in something so intense as the sharing of her unfathomable history.

A mother who was a prostitute who kept having babies (who mysteriously disappeared) encouraged her daughter, Renie, to sit on the steps of an orphanage so she'd be taken care of. How this led from her native Korea to Los Angeles and being placed in an American foster-home nightmare—the succession still makes both my head and heart pound. In this California household, where the family's natural-born kids were treated fairly well, little Renie was relegated to a prison cell of a room. She was barely fed, nor was she allowed to go to the bathroom (instead using what was known in the ghetto as a "slop jar.") She was instructed to always come straight home from school, only to be locked up again. All Renie could do was dream of freedom. Her one hope was through the window, learning the comings and goings of her neighbors. When she grew up a bit, an amazing feat in and of itself, considering the small bits of rice she was fed, she would climb out that window when she knew the neighbors weren't home. She grabbed the keys she spied them placing under the doormat and proceeded to their freezer, frantically scraping ice off the meat, instinctively eating the iron-rich, albeit frozen, food. After cagily learning the neighborhood's in and outs on her way to school, Renie finally made her escape. A Black family found her crying at a bus stop, took her in, and gave this dear soul all the loving kindness she deserved.

While photographing her, it was symbolic that I also helped her get further wings as a flight attendant for Korean Airlines, where she was easily able to travel back to her country of origin and miraculously reunite with some of her family. She met a Korean man, an air marshal (who she would later marry), and so we amicably decided to take a break, which gave me a chance to see if a relationship with Lisa could be in the offing. As with so many incredible women in my life, Renie and I remain best of friends. She is a testament to resiliency by retaining an open heart through any obstacle. You see, while we were dating, I always asked, if not begged, Renie to tell me where her abusive former foster family lived, but she would never, ever do so. Not only was Renie preventing me from getting into trouble, but she had forgiven these people. An ultimate act of selflessness propelled her to have a good life, including being a teacher and a mother of two.

While I was seeing Renie, Lisa's mother unfortunately showed her true colors, trying to push her daughter and me together with outrageous statements like "Why do you have Lisa crying over this 'dragon lady?'"

"Excuse me?" I responded incredulously to such an epithet. "I don't think Lisa should take second place to Renie or nobody. I told her what was going on in my life," I said rather apologetically. And that was it for a minute; regrettably her misguided, conniving doings would be a thread throughout my time with her daughter. When Lisa came on the road with The 5th Dimension, the vibe was perfect, especially because she was an innately good actress and dancer who vicariously enjoyed our musically theatrical outings. But her mother kept pushing, because I guess she thought I had money. "You better get this from him, you better get that!"

Privately, Lisa told me she didn't think she could get pregnant because of some "female situation," so we didn't worry about it. However, when she did, we were so happy to welcome our daughter into the world. I chose her rather unique (for the eighties) name, the mellifluous Ciara. When Lisa and my daughter moved in with me…well, that's when you start finding out about people. I think it's fair to assume her mother never made her clean up anything. For instance, I came home to find an overflowing diaper pail, and she'd be mad if I mentioned it, claiming I was getting on her case. When I came back from the next tour, I found she just bought a bigger diaper pail! We started having these arguments, and she started tripping, seeing other guys and stuff, until finally she ran off with my daughter. Her mother came talking, "Lisa's crazy!"

"Gee, Lisa always said you were the crazy one!" I bit back, sadly thinking how dysfunctional this family was appearing, although Lisa's father, a patient man of Creole descent, was cool. How did he put up with it?

When they all moved to a small ranch in Fresno to care for Lisa's Germanic grandmother, I traveled to see Ciara and took Lisa to dinner one night. "I've been saving from the money you send me, LaMonte. I think I've finally grown up, and we could get back together," she said softly by the glow of candlelight.

In the harsh light of day a week later, I was served with a summons for child support. "The lawyers told my daughter not to speak to you," shrieked her mother when I called.

"That's a bad idea, because all they care about is the money. They don't give a damn about your daughter's relationship with me," was my heartfelt response. So they started going through my assets. They even went after the money I was giving to my mother. At one point, Lisa's mother took Ciara and hid her somewhere. That's when the lawyer I secured, a prominent female attorney who was renowned for handling women's cases but believed in mine, spoke to the judge. Basically out of nowhere, my little girl was driven up to me, leaping out of the car and running into my arms in the presence of my lawyer and the business manager I also found necessary to bring into the proceedings. It sure didn't look like child abuse and all the other bogus stuff Lisa and her team were accusing me of.

Inevitably, Lisa did win the settlement; I had to pay child support, a ridiculous amount of money. She didn't want me to have part-time custody since she could get even more money. Luckily, the judge thought I was due this parental right, so I went to "delightful" Fresno every two weeks or once a month, depending on my touring schedule, to see my daughter for two days at a time. I hated with a passion all that Fresno stood for except my daughter. And Lisa—it's funny, the one person you thought you cared so much about turns out to be the one you least wanna see ever again in your life. That $75,000 in lawyers' fees could have been my daughter's today, and I wrote a letter to Lisa's mother saying as much. "Whatever advice you gave your daughter was bad advice. In worrying about a few dollars, you went after the egg, and you lost the chicken." Maybe my lawyer, the female advocate for women's rights, said it better about Lisa and the entire sordid scenario: "LaMonte, good thing you didn't marry that _____!" Yes, I've omitted the rather tame profanity; Lisa is the mother of my child, after all.

When my daughter got married, Lisa approached me. "I hope we can be friends. I think I made a mistake."

"Yeah, you made a mistake." My voice trailed off. I remembered that forgiveness in life is key. People evolve, too, and ya know, in the long run we wound up being friends. I call, we talk, I tell her a joke or something. What I hold highest, the blessing of our relationship, is Ciara, of course. A Virgo like me, she's full of adventure. Even with making me a grandfather of three and being a supermom to Makayla, Raya, and Shane (aka "L'il Mac"), her aspiration to be a top chef started off well in culinary school. Wonderful departures in catering…and modeling, too, are mainstays for her. As well, she is currently getting her BA in Criminal Justice. Maintaining straight-A grades, not to mention a household full of love, with time to delectably celebrate every event in her children's lives, is "typical Ciara," my daughter of abounding energies. With her kick-ass passion, she also stood up to her grandmother's mind-poisoning ways. "Me and my father have gotten so tight. Say one more thing about him, and you'll never see me again!" I was even prouder when each year I'd pose my daughter in the same leopard-print bathing suit I photographed Lisa in for her mother's appearance in *JET*. The yearly shots I'd take of Ciara in her mom's suit, starting at age one, are in the same vein as measuring a child's height against a wall, but I think this photographic diary of watching my daughter grow up is priceless. When she was eighteen, I had Ciara duplicate the same pose Lisa did for *JET*, and wouldn't you know, the magazine published my photos of mother and daughter, side by side. We'll continue the tradition with my granddaughters.

If I do wrong, I'll always admit to it. Grandma would remind me, "Don't ever blame nobody else for nothing. Think about it. If you wanted out, you wouldn't be part of it, so you have to take responsibility for half of whatever." You get her drift. I agree. I made the decisions, so I have to live with them; that's how I deal with everything. Inevitably, I know I will do right about a situation, and whatever happens, happens, because I sincerely believe right always prevails…it always has, always will. I find the best in everything, and right now I have my daughter out of a certain painful chapter in my life. And Ciara and my wife get along only too well. When she took Ciara to Japan for her high-school graduation present, their bonding-time together stood as a shining example of the affinity between two of the most important women in my life.

After Lisa, I was far removed from having any type of relationship when I met a girl from Washington, DC. That was OK, because it was long distance. Gina had effervescence, and every time we met up, I could tell

I was getting my confidence back with women. She was modeling; I got her in *JET*. She'd meet me at different places The 5th Dimension was performing—all nice, standard fare. Eventually, I was trying to get her to come to California, but she became a queen bee in Ohio, where she'd relocated for a teaching position; Gina just didn't want to move again, and I certainly didn't want to go to Ohio, so it remained a long-distance thing.

One day, I walked into the color lab in Los Angeles where I usually got my pictures developed, and like a vision, this luminously pretty Asian girl appeared behind the counter. Each time I came back, she'd always be smiling. If I came in late, if I needed something in twenty-four hours, her manners in assisting me were impeccable. Another day while conducting business at the lab, I looked up to find all these guys outside, gazing through the window, taking in her beguiling aura. The woman we all wanted to behold was Mieko. Next time I arrived at the lab with my tennis shorts on. "You play tennis? Me too," she said smartly, and we made a date. Mieko was trying so hard to beat me, but I wouldn't let her. I liked her spunk!

Next I announced, "I have a brand new bicycle, do you ride?" and we laughed like kids at the easy pleasure of taking a riding break to buy ice cream and sitting on the curb to eat it. She'd tell me about a boyfriend that wasn't working out, I'd tell her about my long-distance relationship. She'd tell me how to handle girls, I'd tell her how to handle guys. I mentioned The 5th Dimension was performing at the Orange Bowl for New Year's, at halftime. "Is your girlfriend coming?" she inquired. "Yeah, I invited her, she'll be coming down, too," I answered. "Well, I hope you have fun," she grinned but under her breath murmured, "Bullshit." Tickled, I did a double take. "What did you say?" It was so uncharacteristic of her!

And it just started evolving from there. We went out a couple more times, and then I called Gina and said, "That's it, it doesn't seem like this is working." So Mieko and I started dating formally, but with no intention of marriage. The next holiday season came, and The 5th were working for one day on Christmas. I felt it wasn't worth it for Mieko to come join us, but we'd ring in New Year's together. When I found out she called Mama June and flew to St. Louis to spend "the most wonderful time of the year" with her, I thought, "How many girlfriends would go to some-body's mother at Christmastime?" That shed a whole new light on her and my burgeoning feelings.

I had shot Cuba Gooding Jr.'s wedding at a sought-after location in Malibu, and one Sunday shortly after that, Mieko and I went out to the beach. I offered, "Hey, let me show you where I shot Cuba's ceremony. It's such a scenic spot up on the hill, overlooking the bay and all." So we drove up there and were instantly greeted by a wedding planner, who asked if we were interested in getting married there—just like that! "Um, we're just looking around right now," I may have stammered.

"Well, this place is booked for the next year and a half, but I have one day in June that just opened up, and I'll give you a discount!" she pitched. I replied, "I...uh, wait a minute, I said we just came here to look!" Mieko thought aloud, "June, that's your mother's birthday month. That's a good time!"

"Yeah," I said quietly, drifting into the future.

"Do you wanna make a deposit?" added the planner without missing her cue. Later I saw Mr. Gooding and railed at him, jokingly of course, "I'm gonna getcha, man. You're the reason I got married!" I know it was sup-posed to be. That was nearly twenty years ago, June 1, 1995.

I'm thinking again about the people I said "I love you" to. As close as Lisa and I were then, and even with Renie, even Deedee, I honestly don't know if I ever said those three words. We never said that to each other... maybe Deedee, I don't know. Gina, I think I said it once...OK, OK, when

I thought I was in love; I just never really said it! As far as marriage is concerned, I don't believe in a piece of paper. I believe in the person. You can tear up a piece of paper right away. Girls say, "I want a commitment," but what is that if you don't really mean it? You live a commitment, you just don't sign your name on a some paper. Another thing about Mieko— they were putting lots of demands on her about a green card, and she was spending money on legal fees here and there. Then they were putting the screws to all the illegals, making it really hard on them if they didn't register, threatening to deport them, and I said to myself, "No way will she be carried off to Japan," because I knew I was in love. I thought I was.

And then I sat back one night to reflect. I started talking to myself. "Before you make any kind of commitment, where do you go for advice? You go to Grandma." I began to hear her voice across time and space. "LaMonte, if your heart tells you that's the person, scratch it!" She continued with even more kick, "If your mind tells you that's the person, scratch it!"

"So what's left, Grandma?" I could hear my young voice question, transported by my personal oracle.

"LaMonte, if your mind *and* your heart tell you yes, then you got a chance." Her hopeful words rang as clear as a bell. She concluded with gusto, "They don't bullshit each other! Your heart will bullshit you, your mind will bullshit you, but when they start working together, you got a chance!"

"That was really deep, Grandma," I uttered, coming out of my self-imposed hypnosis. If anyone ever put pressure on me to make a commitment, it would work against them. Mieko was so independent, she would never do that to me, even if she were threatened with being put out of the country. It spoke to her integrity and also helped me with my decision to marry her.

And what's our secret? Deedee and I had one argument in eight years. Mieko and I have eight arguments in one day, dumb stuff we end up laughing about later. I have a sense a humor about it right away, she gets mad because I laugh and keep on steppin'. I'll press the point, "You're gonna go around with your lip stuck out? For what? Why can't we just say we agree on something or at least agree to disagree and move on!" But it took her meticulous self a long time. "I can't get rid of it that quick," she'd candidly counter. Now she's learning little by little. I've seen her getting rid of things faster and faster. Even when designing the eclectic décor of our spacious but homey home, it's less a meeting and more a compromise of the minds. And speaking of "homey," or should I say "Homie," Mieko is really quite the character. For no reason at all, she's funny without even realizing it. After I first took her around to meet all my friends, mostly African American men, one day she said out of nowhere, "There are sure a lot of Black people named 'Homes!'"

So close and yet
so far apart,
so sure in mind,
yet uncertain at heart

So begin my lyrics about the star-crossed couple in "A Love Like Ours." Fortunately, with Mieko and myself, there is only certainty of both the mind and the heart.

CHAPTER 10

THE WINDS OF HEAVEN

"...she lives through me..."

Whenever I had finally gotten my first leave from the navy, it was "St. Louis, here I come," where Grandma would be patiently waiting to see me in uniform. It was such a jubilant celebration with my whole family there, like Thanksgiving and Christmas combined. After our heartwarming visit, I took the train back to San Francisco, where I was briefly stationed. I was still grinning from ear to ear as I arrived at the base. I was greeted with, "Don't unpack, McLemore! You need to return to St. Louis, immediately. I'm afraid your grandmother has just died."

I nearly fell on the floor. "Are you talking about *my* grandmother?" I blurted out, not wrapping my brain around the circumstance. In fact, I still can't recall what exactly she passed away from. Stunned into numbness, I could barely hear someone shouting, "Go back now!" It certainly wasn't the voice of God. Then as if divinely led, I tranquilly proceeded to call my family. My voice broke as I choked back tears, and I stated, "I'm not coming back. I'd rather remember Grandma as I left her."

No, I didn't go back. But Grandma continued to be with me, her encouraging smile like the sun itself, warming every single step on my personal highway. Her can-do spirit danced with me like the sparkle in her eyes, embracing me, moving forward with me, achievement by achievement. Everyone tells me she lives through me. I truly believe my grandma is the sweet, merry-eyed, enlightened, loving-without-limits, plain-talkin', straight-shootin' ultimate angel on my shoulder.

CHAPTER 11

STONED SOUL GUMBO

"You ain't gonna make no gumbo with that shit you're getting!"

I think for my next literary destination, I'd like to write a combination cookbook and joke book. I won't tell you the title I have in mind, but as an appetizer, just for you here, I'd like to share some tasty (and not so tasty!) secrets.

Someone had asked if I've been cooking all my life. My reply: "Not yet!" Others have wondered, knowing my penchant for creating gourmet yet down-home recipes, if I got the cooking bug from my mother. Not really, because Mama June was always so busy working, she didn't have the time to prepare meals. Yes, it was Grandma who did most of the cooking in our home. She not only had pretty broad influences, from Cherokee to African American, but she was inventive, too. Like so many of her time with a limited budget, she took whatever was on hand and made a complete meal out of it. What Grandma did with dough alone was phenomenal—a touch of sugar (and love!) and we'd have mouthwatering cookies...and monkey bread, too!

Like with my photography, cooking's a passion for me, and I like making discoveries as I go along. My formula: I think of what I want something to taste like...and I put that ingredient in. If it doesn't turn out right, you ain't gonna hear about it. Well, OK, I'll let you in on one culinary calamity since I've already noted in an earlier chapter the difference between high on the hog vs. low. Isn't it interesting that today, chitterlings or "chitlins," as is more commonly said, cost more than steak and are considered a delicacy? But back in the day, these low on the hog pig intestines were thought to be so funky that no one wanted to cook them in the house or be part of all the labor-intensive cleaning that went with it. My first time preparing them, after a basic turning them inside out and fat removal, I had a light-bulb moment, or so I thought. "Why don't I just throw them in the washing machine...with a touch of Tide to get 'em extra clean!" Before the cycle was up, there was mad foam coming out of the appliance. I yelped, "Those chitlins done messed up my washer!" So I peeled off what was substantially stuck to the cylinder's sides and boiled them in the pot...more foam! There wasn't enough washing I could do; that first attempt at chitlins tasted like acid.

When my kitchen capers do work out right, I try to expand on them, which leads me to my famous "Stoned Soul Gumbo" recipe. I'd love to bring it to you here, as I did on *The Mike Douglas Show* when The 5th Dimension appeared as his guest cohosts for a week in the seventies. A few months after my presentation, Mike personally contacted me saying, "LaMonte, we've never gotten so much viewer mail. Your gumbo set an all-time record!" Before I give you its ecclectic ingredients, let me also share with you the story of how this taste sensation came to me.

Ya know, I always loved gumbo, and I wanted to learn how to cook it, but people from New Orleans, the gumbo capital, are known to basically go to their graves not giving up the recipe! Gumbo can be seafood, chicken, or the kitchen sink. It's bouillabaisse to the fifth power with a big kick of soul. While The 5th Dimension was working in the Big Easy, I must have gone to five or six restaurants to sample the authentic stuff, and I noticed it wasn't as good as I remembered. When I inquired as to why it was tasting so sad, a chef answered, "Things have become so expensive, people are hedging on gumbo ingredients!" Well, I tasted enough to think I had it down. Back in Encino, where the smooth bass singer, Lou Rawls, and I were the first African Americans in our particular neighborhood, I went to shop at a market specializing in fish. I was just as surprised to see a Black man working there as he was intrigued to see me shopping there. So I said hi while I was happily loading mouth-watering things into my pushcart.

The rather old man looked on inquisitively. He piped up, "Excuse me, sir, what are you getting ready to make?"

"I'm gonna make some gumbo," I said with bravado.

He gave my basket a forlorn once-over and replied bluntly, "You ain't gonna make no gumbo with that shit you're getting!"

He took a beat and then proceeded with his stream-of-consciousness confessional. "I'm from Louisiana. In my family are some of the very first people to ever create gumbo. They're all gone now, and I'm the only one who has the recipe. But what good is it if no one can enjoy it?" I could tell he was going to make me an offer. "If you promise to share it with the world, I'll give you the ingredients." Hmm, I don't think he knew I was with The 5th Dimension but probably sensed in some way that I might have culinary clout. Between the stuff I learned from my tastings in New Orleans and this man's divulging things like just the right sausage to put in, I went home to make a pot of gumbo that was so good, I shouted alone in my kitchen, "Boy, look here!" I guess I could have said "Eureka," 'cause for me, it was like finding gold!

I soon was telling my "gumbo discovery story" on *The Mike Douglas Show*, giving the recipe to what would turn out to be the largest response in the show's history. Upon my return to California, I immediately made up a batch and brought a pot to my newfound friend in the fish market as a token of my esteem. But he wasn't there. I asked another man at the counter what happened to my rather mysterious but generous, recipe-giving buddy. He had died. And only two months earlier, he had disclosed his family secret, a delicious tradition. I went home with the pot of gumbo designated for that special soul and ate it all myself. I savored every morsel as an epicurean memorial. And now I bring that recipe to you, in tribute to him.

RECIPE: STONED SOUL GUMBO

In Concert: Everything but the Kitchen Sink!
Starring: Chicken, Sausage, Ham, Okra
Featuring: Lobster, Shrimp, Crab, Mussels, Clams

Soul-ed Out!

Serves 8 to 10

Ingredients:
15 to 20 chicken wings
1 chicken (cut up)
1 hot Andouille (smoked) sausage (cut into quarter slices)
1 cup ham chunks
2 pounds okra (divided)
1 cup green pepper (chopped)
1 cup celery (chopped)
2 medium onions (chopped)
1 garlic clove
5 red pepper pods
2 large cans seasoned tomatoes
1 tablespoon cayenne powder
4 tablespoons (gumbo) file powder (divided)
2, 32 fluid ounce boxes chicken (or beef) stock broth
1 box rice (brown or white)

1 cup olive oil

4 cups flour

1 to 1½ pound Lobster (cut up, left in shell)

1 package shrimp (fresh or frozen)

2 pounds crab (fresh or frozen)

1 package mussels (or clams) (fresh or frozen)

Add or delete the following ingredients to taste—

2 tablespoons hot sauce

3 tablespoons soy sauce

5 bay leaves

Salt and pepper

Preparation:

Microwave sausage for 2 minutes (drain grease)

Fill a plastic bag or bowl with flour, salt and pepper, and cayenne powder

Place cut chicken (including giblets) and wings in seasoned flour—
cover well.

In skillet, cook in olive oil, chopped onions, celery, green pepper
(approximately 5 minutes)

Save olive oil, place onions, celery, and green pepper in large pot*

Fry in a skillet all season-floured chicken in saved olive oil, until at least
browned or half done

Place sausage, ham chunks, and all chicken into large pot*

*one that will accommodate all gumbo ingredients!

Add the roux to large pot—

Secret: the roux is made from the flour of the fried chicken!

Add all chicken (or beef) stock broth, and add water to large pot as
needed to cover all ingredients

Add canned tomatoes, garlic clove, bay leaves, 1 pound of the okra,
pepper pods, cayenne powder, hot sauce, and soy sauce to large pot

Add 2 tablespoons gumbo file to large pot

Gumbo Cooking Instructions:
Slow cook for 1 ½ hours
Slowly stir consistently, so ingredients don't stick but until the sauce sticks to spoon!
After 1 hour, add second pound of okra
Add all seafood in the last 20 minutes

Note: Cook rice separately, according to instructions on box
Remember: This is "Everything But the Kitchen Sink" gumbo but you may add or delete poultry, ham, sausage, or seafood, per your budget and/or to create your own preferred blend!

Serving Suggestion:
Mold rice in a coffee cup, and place in the center of individual soup bowls
Finale: Ladle gumbo over rice molds
Encore: Sprinkle remaining gumbo file powder over each bowl to taste
Serve each bowl on plate (where seafood shells can be placed)
Standing Ovation: Best served with garlic bread!

CHAPTER 12

RIGHT ON!

"I'm just tired, not retired!"

Writing a memoir is like looking at my photos, the ones I prepare for the exhibits of my life's work that are presented at galleries around the country today…even the ones I've put together for you in this book! I'll tell you, it takes time because once I see a couple of pictures, they bring back so many memories, I just have to sit back in the chair! It takes me three days to go over ten pictures, more or less, so you can imagine how long it took to bring you my most important life reflections. They still continue to brim over. I think of the greats I've known. You know, we were very close to Michael Jackson and The Jackson 5. In fact, I still play softball with Jackie Jackson. When the Jacksons came to California in the early seventies, we both lived on the same block in Hollywood, and I'd give the kids a lift up the long, long hill of Queens Boulevard. When they initially moved there, one day this little guy knocked on my door and said, "Sir, can I please have your autograph? Every time I come by, you're never home!" So I signed a photo of The 5th Dimension for him, and after he left, my Hobo Flats roommate of the time said, "That was Michael Jackson!" Such a sense of wonder then…and always, existed in his art. It was a tragic loss when Michael passed away five years ago. We still miss him.

I've already spoken of the incomparable Frank Sinatra, someone I did pinch myself about getting to know. One of the biggest compliments that The 5th Dimension received is that we were the only group he took on the road. We performed in London with him for the Queen, in New York at Radio City with the Rockettes, and on his TV special, "Frances Albert Sinatra Does His Thing." For the latter, Frank became a member of "The 6th Dimension," sporting an exclusive version of our Moon Babies outfits for some "Let's go down by the grapevine" crooning. I think we did three of his retirement parties. He'd retire…then come back stronger each time! We miss him, too.

Oh, dare I share this tidbit? Frank was so kind as to attend The 5th Dimension's opening night at the Americana in New York, and he came backstage postshow accompanied by one of the loves of his life, screen legend Ava Gardner. Now, Frank must have started spending a little too much time chatting up Florence, because a "rebounding" Ava came over to me with a suggestive, "Do you ever get to London, LaMonte? I have a cute little flat there. Here's my number. Why don't you give me a call sometime?" Ironically, months later, there we were at Royal Albert Hall in concert with Sinatra. Everyone who was anyone was there, having a good time as we "Let the Sunshine In"—in the front row I could see Elton John, The Manhattan Transfer, Roger "007" Moore…and there was Ava Gardner, glaring at me with a "You ain't called?" I looked back with an "And I ain't, either!" But I still have her "autograph" and number somewhere in my photographic studio.

As a young photographer, I had the pleasure of taking photos of Nat King Cole and Sammy Davis Jr., too. While I never got to know Nat due to his untimely passing, Sammy became a personal friend over the years; he too loved The 5th Dimension. One night at our Vegas show, he led the crowd in his table-banging, multi-ring flashing, wonderfully enthralled Sammy way by calling for encore after encore. We thought we'd run out of material until we came up with something from left field, our character-driven version of Bobbie Gentry's "Ode to Billie Joe." Marilyn trilled as dramatic narrator while each of the others wailed with comedic flourishes—Florence as Mama, Billy as Papa, Sweets as the brother, and I was "that nice young preacher, Brother Taylor." We killed with that unusual encore, or as I improvized after my solo, "Have mercy!" Sammy was a once-in-a-lifetime star.

Pop-culture icons Don Cornelius, Dick Clark, and Casey Kasem of *Soul Train*, *American Bandstand*, and *American Top 40* fame respectively also were great friends of The 5th Dimension. Don worked so hard in pursuing his dream for Black artists, yet we also had fun together; Dick produced an early nineties recording project for The 5th called "In the House." What a lot of people might not know is Dick, just like Don, had a whole lot of soul. And Casey coined the outstanding phrase, "The 5th Dimension stood in a class by themselves." I'm honored to salute these luminaries who are no longer with us.

Maybe lifting all the luggage over the years while on the road with The 5th Dimension contributed to the situation, but I began having serious back problems, and the doctor offered, "Well, you've never been sixty before!" So I got a talented gentleman to replace me in the group with the thought of coming back after recovering from the pending back surgery. But the doctor also said something that reverberated with me. "Leave while you're on top and enjoy your remaining years." I thought about my family, my wife…I never had enough time to spend with them. So I said, "Call me if you need me," to The 5th Dimension. Now I say, "Just don't call me, because I found out I do nothing well!" My final performance with the group was March 3, 2006.

People ask me what I do for my retirement, and I come back with, "From Monday to Friday, I don't do nothin', and on Saturday and Sunday, I rest!" I also say, "I'm just tired, not retired!" I continue with my photography, of course. Recently, I had the exciting assignment of shooting two years in a row for *Who's Who in Black Las Vegas.* Capturing friends like comedian George Wallace in on-stage action made the work like a day at the beach. And you're never too old to learn something new about the history of the place that you and your wife call home. Did you know Sarann Knight Preddy was the first African American to secure a Nevada gaming license, with which she opened the first interracial Moulin Rouge Casino-Hotel? And Bob Bailey not only hosted the first Black-oriented TV show in Las Vegas, but staged the first lunch counter sit-in at the Fremont Hotel. He even opened a school to train Blacks for gaming jobs. It was meaningful to portray these trailblazers—especially in light of Ms. Preddy's recent passing—for the prestigious annual tribute guide produced by the ambitious Wendy Welch. What else? I'm writing, as you can see. And I've been playing ball with a team of very hip seniors here in Las Vegas. I played 170 games last year. That's more than the majors; they only play 162! We're on the field in the sun and even the snow.

The 5th Dimension traveled the world many times over, but all we saw were airports, concert halls, and hotels, and then we'd be back on the plane. So now I get to fulfill my bucket list and "go where I wanna go" to the places I've really wanted to see. My wife and I are taking our frequent flyer miles and running all over the world from Antarctica to Jakarta. We just came back from the Amazon jungle, out where there was no electricity. I didn't know if she could hang, but she handled it better than I did. Eating dinner by candlelight, after fishing for and catching the rather bony but tasty piranha we deliciously prepared, I winked to Mieko. "I hope we taste as good to them as they do to us!"

I also started this celebrity softball team with Little Anthony Gordine, my cousin Robert DeBlanc, who performed with Marvin Gaye and is now with Little Anthony and The Imperials, Harry Elston of The Friends of Distinction, Bubba Knight of Gladys Knight and The Pips, and Sonny Turner of The Platters. We named it The Flashbackz, with a Z. We started it to raise money for charity, and then it developed into something more, with Gladys Knight and Mary Wilson as our team cheerleaders. When Gladys invited The Flashbackz to perform at her Las Vegas show to surprise her husband for his birthday, we got together to rehearse, and the camaraderie was sensational as we shared stories and worked on songs from each group. We put our little tuxes on and went out there and just turned the house out! Some agents in the audience expressed interest, but I said, "Man, I'm trying to retire!" OK, so we trademarked the name and took the press photos. Then everyone got busy with their own groups. But if we ever take The Flashbackz show on the road, it will be like a nouveau version of The Rat Pack, or as people affectionately say, The Black Pack. They have all these impersonators out there, but hey, we're the originals!

Speaking of original, a few years ago I had the idea to bring the taste of good ole southern cuisine to Vegas, and along with other celebrity partners, our restaurant Catfish Alley became one of the first African American-owned businesses on the new Las Vegas strip. Our food was scrumptious, and we featured entertainment, too, but the endeavor was rather short-lived due to extenuating circumstances. However, as with all my firsts on my life mission, I felt called to do this and I'm gratified by what we were able to achieve.

People have asked me what I'd have done if I didn't have a life in baseball, photography, or music. Well, besides developing *Elegant* magazine or orchestrating Catfish Alley, I'd have been a comedian, plain and simple. Not the class clown type, mind you, who essentially rabble-rouses, but the one who is actually out there doing it. I guess that's why with The 5th Dimension, I'd be their designated comedic spokesman in our stage shows. Three of my biggest influences in this regard were Bill Cosby, Richard Pryor, and Redd Foxx. They were not only drop-dead funny, but they knew how to tell stories with an underlying message. That's what made them all good actors, too. When Bill Cosby and The 5th Dimension were both playing dates in Atlantic City, we casually invited him to play softball with us. He and I hit it off and remained friends from then on. Bill was nice to people but naturally self-protective; however, we shared an easygoing rapport. We never discussed the standards of excellence both he and The 5th Dimension subscribed to, but there was a quiet understanding as symbolized on *The Cosby Show* itself. Right on the Huxtable family's coffee table sat my photographic portfolio.

At the time of this writing, old and new allegations about Bill Cosby have surfaced in the media. I have only known Bill as a person of sincerity. Anything to the contrary would be something difficult for me to wrap my mind around. I pray for the best resolution of the situation, for all parties concerned.

Richard Pryor and I got to be real crazy friends, and I say it that way because I knew how he was. Here's an example. Upon completing the interior decoration of my house in Encino, I held a small dinner party. The guests included this bourgeois couple. Actually the wife was one of the decorators, the husband was a doctor. Just as we were getting ready to have an after-dinner toast, Richard called. "Do I hear a party goin' on? I've got Pam Grier (*Foxy Brown*) and Cleavon Little (*Blazing Saddles*) with me. We'll be right over!" I had no time to say, "Wait, Richard, it's an intimate gathering!"

They arrived just as we began playing a seemingly sedate game of backgammon, and to this day I can't recall what Pam or Cleavon did. But Richard insisted on joining right in with a purposely silly observance: "Wow, you got white people here, too!" The doctor of the couple was shrewd. We were playing for money, and he let Pryor win a few games before it became dog-eat-dog. Soon Richard was on a losing streak, in it for six hundred dollars. He mischievously exploded, "I ain't got no six hundred bucks to give you, Doc. I'm just gonna have to suck your *johnson* instead!" "N-n-no, you don't have to. You owe me nothing," said the doctor, half out the door with his wife in tow. Later she called, peeved. "LaMonte, how could you do that to us?" I responded, "I'm so sorry, I didn't know that Richard Pryor—"

"Wait"—she stopped me—"Was that *the* Richard Pryor? Well, that makes all the difference!"

I went way back with Redd Foxx of *Sanford and Son* fame to St. Louis, where he'd be playing teeny comedy clubs. Red would be out back, taking a cigarette break, and I'd go inquire if whatever little singing group I was with at the time could do a song. His line was, "I'm not letting you on stage, messing up my pension!" But he generously did, introducing us with "Here they are, fresh out of Las Vegas…" We had barely been out of our living rooms! He'd remind me of that years later when he and The 5th Dimension would both be playing Las Vegas. "Man, I'm so proud of you." He beamed and added, "I'm getting ready to do this TV sitcom, and I'd like you, LaMonte, to try out for the part of my son." But I sadly declined because of The 5th Dimension's busy time commitments. I do think Redd and I would have made for a great father/son team. When *Sanford and Son* came out, I asked Redd, "How come you named your son 'Lamont'?" And he gave me his trademark laugh. "Heh, heh, heh!"

So many people stop me each and every day to ask about my 5th Dimension cohorts. We are forever linked. We are family. I have much respect for my "brother," Billy Davis Jr. He was candid about his recovery from alcoholism in the memoir he and his wife, Marilyn McCoo, wrote a few years back; he has been sober for decades. Billy remains one of our greatest Soul singers. The man we sometimes called "June Bug" and I still chuckle about a "haunting" early Hobo Flats escapade that could probably be fodder for one of those ghost story TV shows. But what I really want to acknowledge is that presently, Billy is also a stirring pastor with his ministry, Soldiers for the Second Coming. And who in the world does not like, if not revere, Ms. McCoo, a diva in the best sense of the word. She will always be the essence of class and loveliness personified. While her recorded vocal solos are the definition of artistry, her in-person song stylings today are impossibly better than ever. Marilyn, along with her hubby, is a person of deep Christian faith. Mieko and I never miss a chance to see Marilyn McCoo and Billy Davis Jr. in concert as a duo…sounding all silky, soulful, and utterly astounding. They are now celebrating forty-five years of marriage.

We also never miss a chance to see Florence LaRue continue to reach new heights leading The current 5th Dimension or when she performs her one-woman show, "Just As I Am." If I were casting a Broadway musical on The 5th Dimension story, I would have Ms. LaRue play her younger self. She never, ever ages! But what is it about beautiful women that can make some insecure? I don't blame Florence for the little disagreements we've had over time. I mean, the two of us navigated The 5th Dimension together for over forty-one years before I retired. Soon Florence will be celebrating five decades with the group! There was a lot of weight on her diminutive shoulders, especially after Marilyn and Billy departed. Florence kept The 5th afloat magnificently, but sometimes she just wouldn't let me do my share. When you're telling the photographer how to light Black people on stage, well, it can be pretty disconcerting. I mean, I've been professionally lighting people of color all my life, and no, we don't get washed out in blue spotlights! I guess I have to laugh…and extend my admiration, too. Hands down, Florence LaRue is the consummate entertainer. She dazzles her audience and truly touches hearts. And did you know she has an uncanny gift for not only knowing her musical part, but everyone's? I understand her, and then again I don't, but I'll always love her. She too is deserving of the title, diva. As well, she's a woman of great Christian faith.

I also acknowledge the group's Music Director of many years who began playing with us at the tender age of eighteen. Ron Feuer is a gifted young man who loyally remains on tour with The 5th Dimension to this day (along with John Lewis on drums and J. V. Collier on bass) among his other musical endeavors.

And then there's our Sweet Man. It's funny, because the four of us could walk on one side of the street and Sweets would be on the other, and people would run over to Ron Townson because they recognized his authoritative yet adorable, one-of-a-kind look more than the rest of us put together. Ron was a man of supposedly traditional values who'd chide Florence for wearing her trendy micro-miniskirts. "If you were my wife, I wouldn't allow you to wear them!" "Well, that's why you're not my husband!" she'd wisecrack back. He'd tell me that nudity in film was not appropriate. However, he seemed to see nothing wrong with certain violent movies of the time, that made for popular viewing, especially by males. I'd call him out with, "You mean you can shoot a breast, but you can't kiss it?" All good-natured verbal sparring aside, it was abundantly clear that Ron took the utmost pride in his contribution to The 5th Dimension and to music history as a whole. We lost Ronald in the summer of 2001. The Original 5th Dimension will never have a concert reunion again without our beloved Sweet Man. People keep asking. But Ron "Sweets" Townson is irreplaceable, period.

But that's not the end of the story, the group's or my own. As one of the most popular vocal groups of the Rock 'n' Roll era, The 5th Dimension will always be remembered for our greatest contribution—we joined people together by the "joyful noise" we made. I think we provided a comforting if not pleasantly inspiring diversion during our country's unsettled days of the Vietnam War and the aftershocks of the assassinations of Dr. Martin Luther King and Robert Kennedy, and that's pretty heavy. We also opened a lot of doors on TV and in Las Vegas. If you can imagine it, of The Temptations, The Four Tops, Smokey Robinson and The Miracles, even with all their hits, only two Black singing groups headlined in the main Vegas showrooms in the late sixties: The Supremes and The 5th Dimension. And we were making money, so someone said, "If the other Black groups can do that, too, well then, give them a shot!"

I may be the least religious of us all, but the members of The 5th Dimension were always thankful—I mean seriously grateful—to God for our opportunities. We had no prima donnas...we were all touchable. Today, whether on YouTube, on CD reissues or compilations like *The Essential*, *The Ultimate*, or *Playlist: The Very Best of The 5th Dimension*, and on terrestrial or Internet radio, our authentic sound prevails, so that emerging artists, as well as audiences old and new, can embrace it. I'm noticing younger people are discovering and even researching The 5th Dimension. This is why the *Forever 5th Dimension* blog is so important. Knowing of established artists, too, who cite our influence like John Legend, Earth, Wind and Fire, Swing Out Sister (who covered "Stoned Soul Picnic"), De La Soul (who sampled "Black Patch"), Vanessa Williams (who covered "One Less Bell," and told of how her family would gather 'round the TV to watch The 5th Dimension, while she was growing up), and many more, is always rewarding.

And I laughed out loud when the multi-gifted Pharrell Williams of "Happy" fame, gave this euphoric compliment in a recent edition of *Ebony*, reflecting on his upbringing and influences: "And let me tell you, LaMonte McLemore, who took all the *JET* 'Beauty of the Week' pictures with all the bad, finest, finest, finest sisters in bathing suits? Good Lawd!" Back atcha, my brother. I can't tell you how many people mention to me that the mega hit of the millennium, "Happy" sounds like it could be a 5th Dimension tune, and that makes me happy!

"A Change is Gonna Come" is a classic that Billy led The 5th Dimension in so passionately. Indeed it has come...in certain ways. I surely never thought I'd see our first Black president. Or maybe I did. In every line of "A Love Like Ours" is personal freedom, in "The Singer" is an artist's pathos, in "Stoned Soul Picnic" is unadulterated delight, in "Let the Sunshine In" is glorious expectation, in "Up-Up and Away" is eternal optimism, all manifesting a type of harmonious unconditional love that has surpassed my wildest dreams. In every "Love Line" of my life is what Grandma and Mama June wished—if not predicted—for me. In every ball I've pitched, photo I've taken, song I've performed, and joke I've told is the promise of tomorrow. I said at the beginning, I never plan to make a friend I don't intend to keep. So now that we're stuck, I say, "Right on!"

EPILOGUE

OK, I'm back! I told you we're stuck, but just for a little extra time here, promise! And yes, I'm thinking of *The Magic Garden* album where Jimmy Webb wrote us that masterful prologue and epilogue, "Have You Tried Love?" I think my personal slant is in the ballpark.

I had a relative named Daisy Singleton, whose brother married my sister, Merilyn. Daisy worked as a nurse in one of those retirement homes for the wealthy. One day her car broke down, and I was asked to pick her up at "the home." I arrived early, and there she was, pushing this elderly yet distinguished, gray-haired white man in a wheelchair. Daisy introduced us. "This is 'Mr. So and So,' and you can talk with him, LaMonte, while I get my hat and coat."

I piped up, "How you doin', sir?" and he reacted with, "What can I do for her?"

I inquired, "What do you mean?"

He revealed in a kind but emphatic tone, "She is one of the nicest people I've ever known, but she won't tell me what I can do for her."

I tried to be matter-of-fact. "Well, I came to pick up Daisy because her car broke down," and lo and behold, a few months later, he bought her a car.

Then he asked me, "Are you a millionaire?"

I responded with earnest incredulity, "I'm just out of the service; I'm on unemployment and drawing welfare!"

He asked, "Young man, how would you like to be prosperous before you leave here?"

I laughed. "Who wouldn't?"

He went on, "I was the president of a large national candy company that I just sold…and I'm a multimillionaire because of it. Oh, but I have multiple sclerosis and am paralyzed from the waist down. So if you can do one thing for me, I'll make you a rich man tonight."

I went along. "Yes, sir, what can I do for you?"

He answered in a nearly pastoral cadence, as his wheelchair became a pulpit of sorts. "All you have to do is change places with me. I'll give you all my multimillions. All you have to do is be paralyzed and sit in this wheelchair while I walk out of here totally healthy. Will you do it?"

Stunned, I summoned an "I don't think so."

His final words echo to this day. "See, you came in here a millionaire and didn't even realize it."

As I walked out of the nursing home with Daisy, I said, "Damn!" After that encounter, I never looked at material things the same way. Yep, another life-changing moment, one that sealed the phrase, "If I have my health, I have my wealth."

When we took Mama June to Paris for her ninetieth birthday, it was because she announced, "I'm not gonna wait till I'm ninety-one!" While we tried to sneak past her room one night to go to a disco, she opened the door and imp-ishly grinned, "Hey, don't y'all leave me!" For her ninety-fifth, we took her to Cabo San Lucas, and the airline lost her walker, as usual. We got to the hotel and requested a wheelchair and got an old rickety one with no rub-ber on the rims. As we were pushing her down those dusty Baja roads in that raggedy chair, concerned for my mother's comfortable ride, she chirped up, "LaMonte, are *you* all right?" At this writing, Mama June has just turned one hundred years young. Her memory is better than yours and mine put to-gether, she's as sharp as a tack, and we are blessed that she ain't thinking about leaving here anytime soon. Marilyn and Billy, who attended her grand centen-nial celebration, put it well: "Mama June is one of the true gems in our lives. She's always been full of joy, love, and acceptance. She is the only remaining parent of any of the original members of The 5th Dimension and is a treasured part of the group's lives." A dear friend of mine put it another way: "Mama June is not only lovely but brilliant. She possesses a warm godly light—not only coming from inside but surrounding her—that is simply breathtaking when in her presence." That's my mama, and I get rather choked up about her, so I'm glad they said it for me!

My sister Joan Truelove ("Joanie") also has a glow. A sweet angel, she, along with my niece, Felicia, Merilyn's daughter, so selflessly care for Mama June today. My mother still resides in her spacious yet cozy St. Louis home. I'm thinking back to about four years ago, when The 5th Dimension received its star on the St. Louis Walk of Fame. To have family, friends we grew up with, and special fans attend the induction ceremony was like a carnival in the city where Billy, Ron, and I all grew up. Mama June was there, but I couldn't help but miss my sidekick, Duck. He passed away of a brief illness a few years earlier. Duck is fondly remembered as the road manager for The 5th Dimension in the early days. At his funeral I stated with emotion, "People always referred to Duck as 'LaMonte's brother.' For now on, I am known as 'Duck's brother.'" At the Walk of Fame, I also missed my sister Merilyn. If you met her, you'd fall hope-lessly in love. Even a party would come to a slow-motion halt upon my big sister's grand entrance. Alluring in looks and attitude, Merilyn owned a beauty shop and developed a pomade-type hair straightener that was highly popular. But I think it was the constancy of having to deal with perfecting its chemical formula, including lye, which caused her terminal cancer. Like Mama June, Merilyn was an accepting soul; for instance, she fully embraced Lynn, who worked in her salon and had a male-to-female sex change at a time when it was highly uncommon. In fact, it may have been one of the first operations of its kind. Fittingly, it was Lynn's expertise in makeup and hair that made Merilyn beautiful again at her funeral.

If you Google around, you may have noticed sites that say, "LaMonte has two children, a daughter and son." While Ciara is my natural daughter, Darin is my son by adoption. Let's just say, a very special young lady had become an unwed mother at a time it was not readily acceptable. When I went to see her newborn at the hospital, and he gripped my hand so tightly, it was a love-at-first-touch moment. Such a feeling came over me that I knew in my bones I just had to become his dad by adoption. Today, Darin is a fine young man, working in the recording industry; we share mutual respect and admiration. And I wish to mention another promising young man, Donnie McLemore, who is Duck's son. My nephew carries on the McLemore tradition of innovation with his work in the field of financial management as a wealth specialist adviser. Ya know, come to think of it, maybe I was predestined to step up with Darin; it's exactly what my mother's brother, L. C. Shaver, did to fill in for my father's absence in our growing up years. L. C. will always be remembered as a father, uncle, and brother to us…he was everything. He could be tough in his defensive way, like the time he showed up to Duck's school, guns ablaze, to put some sense into the teacher who violently snatched off my little brother's ahead-of-its-time earring. L. C., aka "Two-Gun Pete," schooled my bro's blood-drawing prof in a way that was better than a Clint Eastwood movie. He had the other students jumping out of windows to avoid the chance of ricocheting bullets! Now, I'm all for "Cease Fire," so I'm letting you know that I think L. C.'s bark was worse than his bite. I got my sense of humor from him, and we bonded even more strongly as I got older. He'd say, "LaMonte, when you grow up, you're gonna go down many paths. Just be sure you have your shoes on!"

I'm also thinking of my close friend Richard Roundtree, who began as an *Ebony* Fashion Fair model before he starred in the movie blockbuster, *Shaft*. As that supercool detective, he became the first Black male sex symbol. At the start of his pop-cultural recognition, he was staying with me at Hobo Flats, since his road to fame was not yet paved with gold. Among the many events he was invited to, it was of utmost importance that he look his best at the Academy Awards ceremony. So as slick as Shaft, Richard scoped shoes from myself, a tie from Duck, and a suit from Harry Elston. And he got voted best dressed man that year! A number of years later he had breast cancer, from which he recovered, and he courageously became a spokesman for the condition, taking the stigma away from men dealing with this. I'll always respect Richard, for he, too, is a man who stepped up.

And a further shout-out goes to Harry, who started off with me in The Hi-Fi's and later had his fame with The Friends of Distinction. He wound up being my Hobo Flats roommate on and off for twenty years. Married, divorced, girlfriend, and married again, his spirit of fun is actually a generous gift to me. And who else can get my wife, Mieko, talkin' in soulful slang?

I think you can tell by now, with all the achievements and accolades The 5th Dimension and I have garnered, I will never forget Hobo Flats. I would invite all the "refugees" to come and stay—not only Harry and Richard, but members of The Temptations, Earth, Wind and Fire…we'd pool our slim funds together, the girls would come around on the weekend, and we'd have more pure good times than anyone. Of course, the members of The 5th Dimension gathered at Hobo Flats early on, too; Marilyn and Billy first met there and credit me with introducing them. I can still hear our collective laughter as distinct as our five-part musical harmonies. But there was something serious behind the laughs. You'll recall that Hobo Flats wasn't so much a place but a feeling—of great expectations anchored by resourcefulness to untether our metaphoric "beautiful balloon." Even more, Hobo Flats reminds me of the biggest lesson of all that Grandma taught me, that I hold highest on her greatest hits list. It's what everyone I wrote about in this epilogue, in this entire memoir, brings to mind, too. It's the foundation for everything I do, and yes, it's simple: I believe we're only in this world to help one another. So I guess, in other words, "Have You Tried Love?"

DISCOGRAPHY OF THE 5TH DIMENSION

THE ALBUMS

Up-Up and Away, 1967, Soul City

The Magic Garden, 1968, Soul City

Stoned Soul Picnic, 1968, Soul City

The Age of Aquarius, 1969, Soul City

The 5th Dimension: Portrait, 1970, Bell

Love's Lines, Angles and Rhymes, 1971, Bell

LIVE!, 1971, Bell

Individually and Collectively, 1972, Bell

Living Together, Growing Together, 1973, Bell

Soul and Inspiration, 1974, Bell

Earthbound, 1975, ABC

Star Dancing, 1978, Motown

High on Sunshine, 1978, Motown

In the House, 1995, Click

THE TOP 40 POP
AND R&B SINGLES
(REPORTED BY BILLBOARD)

Song, Date Charted (Pop), Pop Peak, Weeks (on chart), R&B Peak, Label

Go Where You Wanna
2/4/67, Pop 16, 7 Wks, Soul City

Up-Up and Away*
6/17/67, Pop 7, 10 Wks, Soul City

Paper Cup
12/9/67, Pop 34, 1 Wk, Soul City

Carpet Man
2/24/68, Pop 29, 5 Wks, Soul City

Stoned Soul Picnic
6/22/68, Pop 3, 12 Wks, R&B 2, Soul City

Sweet Blindness
10/26/68, Pop 13, 6 Wks, Soul City

California Soul
1/11/69, Pop 25, 6 Wks, Soul City

Aquarius/Let The Sunshine In^
3/15/69, Pop 1 (6 Wks), 16 Wks, R&B 6, Soul City

Workin' On A Groovy Thing
8/9/69, Pop 20, 7 Wks, R&B 15, Soul City

Wedding Bell Blues
10/4/69, Pop 1 (3 Wks), 14 Wks, R&B 23, Soul City

Blowing Away
1/24/70, Pop 21, 6 Wks, Soul City

Puppet Man
5/2/70, Pop 24, 5 Wks, Bell

Save The Country
 6/27/70, Pop 27, 5 Wks, Bell

One Less Bell to Answer
11/21/70, Pop 2 (2 Wks), 15 Wks, R&B 4, Bell

Love's Lines, Angles and Rhymes
3/13/71, Pop 19, 8 Wks, Bell

Never My Love
10/2/71, Pop 12, 9 Wks, Bell

Together Let's Find Love
1/29/72, Pop 37, 3 Wks. R&B 22. Bell

(Last Night) I Didn't Get To Sleep At All
4/22/72, Pop 8, 13 Wks, R&B 28, Bell

If I Could Reach You
9/30/72, Pop 10, 12 Wks, Bell

Living Together, Growing Together
2/10/73, Pop 32, 4 Wks, Bell

Honorable Mention—
A Change Is Gonna Come/People Gotta Be Free
2/28/70, Pop 60, 4 Wks, Bell

Love Hangover
4/3/76, Pop 80, 4 Wks, R&B 39, ABC

---

*Winner of four Grammy® awards for The 5th Dimension
^Winner of two Grammy® awards for The 5th Dimension

GRANDMA GERTRUDE'S TOP 20 GREATEST HITS

Here's a review of Grandma's wise sayings, with a couple of extras for good measure. See how many come to mind as you go about your daily life!

20. To get 100 percent out of something, try putting 100 percent in.

19. The only time you have an argument is when you try to make someone else wrong.

18. You have only one life and one body. Take care of them.

17. There's no such thing as a competition until *you* walk in. (In other words, be prepared, take a risk and step up with self-confidence.)

16. Love, like fire, needs fuel.

15. Do you always want to be right or be happy?

14. To have friends, you have to be one.

13. Love is an open hand. (Grandma would have birds eating seeds literally out of her hand; generosity and kindness are key.)

12. Find the good in everything that seems to be bad.

11. You can only do a day's work in one day.

10. Take the gray out of your life and live ten years longer. (Translation: Be direct with your words—no beating around the bush!)

9. Opportunity always knocks twice; the second time just ain't for you!

8. Never look down on a man unless you are tying to pick him up.

7. If you trace the path of boredom, it will always lead back to you.

6. There's no such thing as problems, only "situations."

5. Simplicity is perfection at its finest.

4. Whenever you seek revenge, you dig two graves…one for the offender, one for yourself.

3. The sun rises and sets for everyone. We're the only ones who screw it up in between.

2. If God can forgive, who are we not to?

1. We are only in this world to help one another.

Bonus—
If your mind *and* your heart tell you yes, then you've got a chance at love.

LAMONTE McLEMORE ACKNOWLEDGES...

In the spirit of my grandmother's and my mother's generosity, if your name was mentioned somewhere in this memoir, my book is sincerely dedicated to you, too.

However, there are so many people who have been a beautiful part of my life, it was impossible to include all of them in one book. Therefore, I want to acknowledge you here. I firmly believe people's paths cross to bring inspiration we may find at first sight or may realize later. Either way, their light shines in our soul, making the heart sing forever.

Thank you to all, for the love, joy, and golden memories, and for letting me be a part of your life, too.

Larry Armstrong

Kenny Bates

Janet "Janet Janet" Bissett

David Gest

Steve Rosenblum

Pat Huff and Keno

Chuck Johnson

Dee VanNess

Jane Tani

Ben Sumpter

Bill Bateman

Joel Durham

Maria DeSouza

Clarence Collins

Miles Robinson

Ryuji Iijima

Dennis Turner

Richard Coleman

Ed Edwards, Jay Bird Depland,
and Roger Witherspoon—my "other brothers"

Susan Munao

James Watson

Jackki Davis

Veronica Davis

Maurice Renaldi

Misty Beck

Mike Gibson

Phyllis Ellis

Ralph DeBlanc

Melody Williams

Stony Gillespie

Wanda A'cuna

Kanna Kuna

Anna Wood

Benny Clay

Charles Glenn

Johnny Cade

George Harpes

Sonny Charles

Keni Burke

Chris Hutchinson

Helen Funai

LeRoy Graham

Rick Harris

John White

Earl Woodridge

Ron Hare

Mike Tatsui and Christopher Halenbeck

Judy Millet Scott

Ronneane English

Nannette "SC" Okonkwo

Daphne Dumas

Henry Kenji

Pat Pennix

Juanita Moore

Terry Jones

Avel Williams

Loretta Butler

Kim Savage

Carolyn Paddock

Geno Henderson

John Wood

Sonny Porter

Mary Gilmore

Robert Miller

Lloyd Taylor

David Thomas

David O'Haire

Anthem Senior Softball Team

All my "Catfish" investors

To Robert-Allan Arno aka "Rev. Arno"—There is no one better to tell my story; we were destined for this confab of a lifetime. Your abounding energy over the years, "making it perfect" for The 5th Dimension legacy and me, never ceases to amaze! Mieko and I love and respect you.

In memory of Ron "Sweets" Townson

ROBERT-ALLAN ARNO ACKNOWLEDGES...

With deep appreciation and affection, I honor all of you who are truly God's special blessings to me:

LaMonte McLemore—We had the time of our lives. You are a kindred spirit and a cherished brother like no other; my parents, Annette and Robert Esposito, for your loving hearts; Phyllis McGrane; Mama June, Mieko McLemore, and Ciara McLemore; Marilyn McCoo and Billy Davis, Jr.—my angels; Florence LaRue—from the heart; Bones Howe—a mentor; Kyle Townson and the Townson family; Johnny Mathis; Nancy Sinatra; Neil Sedaka; Otis Williams; Vanessa Williams; Pharrell Williams; Randall Jeffries; Jeremy Holiday; Allan Sniffen, and Bob Radil of Rewound Radio; Bill Quinn of Metromedia Radio; Sylvia Flanagan; Ashley Vincent-LeBlanc; Sara Ann Zola and the Team, including Jeannie, Jesse, and Jamie; Ellen Cohen; Bob Marks; Jeffrey Graham; Rob "Broham" Clark; Elsie Urbina; Molly Gallentine; Kathy "KK" Bretz; Sharon Gordon; Annette Aiken; Doug Bushell; Julie Anne Ramos; Andy Gard; Kathy Berenson; Peter Purpura; Tamar Shapiro; Cathryn Taylor; Karen Lehman; Richard Winslow; Isabel Howe; Joan Bogden; Renie Q; Jamie and Jacqueline Bassel; Nazir Nasir; Nhojj; Anton Nimblett; Rasaan Bourke; David Pendleton; Donald Durant; Cleve Douglass; Jayson Cross; Joyce Wright Pierce; Patrice Morris; Dorothea Joyce; Dennis Lambert; Laurel Massé; Wilma Mott; my church family at Saint Malachy's—The

Actor's Chapel; my TV family at The Sunday Mass; the dedicated fans at Forever 5th Dimension, including Susie Paige, Susan Aglio, Renée Armstead, Loretta Sorensen, Emiko Ikeda, Martha Vink, Patricia Correa, Deniserose Torres, Kenneth Green, John Estes, David Roberson, Douglas C. Charles, Dale Kocik, Alain Baptiste, Gary Holland, Antonio Pereira, and Brian Medoro. In memory of Mary Bivona; the Rev. Dr. Melvin C. Walker, The Gospel Ambassador; and Grandmas Concetta and Gertrude.

LaMONTE McLEMORE

For interview, public appearance,
or photographic exhibit
requests, please contact:
lmphotog@cox.net

9 780692 307366